The ENTREPRENEUR

MAINSTREAM VIEWS & RADICAL CRITIQUES

SECOND EDITION

ROBERT F. HÉBERT
ALBERT N. LINK

PRAEGER

New York
Westport, Connecticut
London

Library of Congress Cataloging-in-Publication Data

Hébert, Robert F.
    The entrepreneur : mainstream views and radical critiques / Robert
F. Hébert, Albert N. Link : foreword by G. L. S. Shackle.—2nd ed.
        p. cm.
    Bibliography: p.
    Includes index.
    ISBN 0-275-92810-1 (alk. paper)
    1. Entrepreneurship—History. I. Link, Albert N. II. Title.
HB615.H34   1988
338'.04'09—dc19   87-38188

Library of Congress Catalog Card Number: 87-38188
ISBN: 0-275-92810-1

First published in 1988

Praeger Publishers, One Madison Avenue, New York, NY 10010
A division of Greenwood Press, Inc.

Printed in the United States of America

♾️

The paper used in this book complies with the Permanent
Paper Standard issued by the National Information Standards
Organization (Z39.48—1984).

10 9 8 7 6 5 4 3 2 1

*FOR
DIANE
AND
CAROL*

CONTENTS

FOREWORD
by G. L. S. Shackle

Can a list which begins with the dramatist, the symphonist, and the mathematician come naturally and fittingly at last to the business man, the entrepreneur? All of these are *originators*. The world which such a man senses around him may be in itself the same sort of world as presents itself to all of us. But what it means to him is different. It is for the *original mind* a sesame of untold riches of suggestion. All perception is no doubt an act of interpretation, of finding in, or injecting into sense-impressions a meaning, the collating with them of numberless memories of experience, the seeing in them of *possibilities*. This is in its own degree an act of origination. This same activity of thought, but at an enormously enriched, intensified and out-ranging degree, is what marks the creative writer, composer or theoretician, and it is what marks the entrepreneur.

The business man commands *resources*. Are these just material objects or collections, or money in the bank, or human colleagues with gifts of intellect and skill which they can offer as collaborators? All these things, even the skills, are in themselves *inert*. In themselves they are meaningless. It is when they are seen as means, as *potentiae*, as capable of uses, that they become resources. What is the indispensable psychic act which gives them meaning as resources? It is imagination, the ultimate creative act of thought in which men are tempted, with some excuse, to find their apotheosis, to see themselves as plenipotentiaries of divine power. Imagination is what informs the deeds of poet and symphonist, of the inventor of mathematics at the utmost limit of subtlety, of the sculptor and painter, and of the creator of a business. Yet this last exploit needs an extra gift. He must have nerve. He must commit himself, he must stake his chips. For no man can know what will be the sequel of his chosen act.

To admit that we do not know what will be the course of our affairs if we do this, or if we do that, goes somewhat against the grain. Yet if we claim that our choice of one course of action rather than another *makes a difference*, we are claiming that choice is an act of *absolute origination*, that it can have effects not implicit in antecedents. If so, there is no foreknowing what a choice-to-come will be, by inference from its antecedents. Choices-to-come, made by ourselves or others, cannot be foreknown. Yet they will have effects, and they will affect to some greater or less degree the sequel of our present act. Then, in choosing that present act, we are in the nature of things in some respects blind. The entrepreneur is a man whose characteristic act is a gamble on his imagination. Of course, the business man uses reason and knowledge. He sees principles in the natural universe, he has insights into human powers and propensities. He can form judgements of what can come about, he cannot know uniquely what *will* come about.

What can his choice of action do? What can it do *in the present*, what difference can there be between one thought-commitment and another? One use of his resources will *exclude from possibility* some histories-to-come which in the abstract he can imagine. Another use of his resources will remove the obstacle, but impose one on some members of a different skein of imagined sequels. Let us then define enter-prise. It is action in pursuit of the imagined, deemed possible. Any course of action must expose the chooser to numberless different sequels, rival hypotheses, some desired and some counter-desired. To say this is simply to say that freedom to create history entails unknowledge of what history will be created. The entrepreneur is a maker of history, but his guide in making it is his judgement of possibilities and not a calcu-lation of certainties.

PREFACE TO THE
SECOND EDITION

This is a revised and updated version of our previous attempt (Hébert and Link 1982) to chronicle the conceptual history of the entrepreneur. To practicing economists, supply and demand are the commonplaces of everyday life, and such matters intrude even upon the writing of books. In preparing this revision for publication, we again confronted both kinds of questions. From the supply side we asked, Why write such a book? Recognizing that authorship itself is an entrepreneurial act, it can be said that all books are written to satisfy the (known) desires of the authors who write them and the (anticipated) desires of the readers who read them. The motivation to write this book is simple: our intellectual curiosity about a subject that has increasingly come into economic vogue during this decade.

The concept of the entrepreneur admits of no single, accepted definition in the literature of economics or its related disciplines. As a consequence, economic theory and policy dealing with entrepreneurship are bound to be ambiguous. The premise of this book is that we cannot hope to understand, even moderately well, the present state of the subject without knowing the past ideas and circumstances that inevitably shape both present and future. Therefore, this study is first and foremost an exercise in intellectual history.

From the demand side we asked, Who will want to read this book? Naturally we cannot anticipate fully the unknowable nature of its future readership, but we hope the book appeals to those who share our intellectual curiosity about an important subject, and who would therefore welcome a summary statement of its historical evolution. Although not directed exclusively to them, we feel this book will be of special interest to students—especially those who are deprived by modern university curricula of historical perspectives on important subjects that shape our present and future lives.

This is not a 'how to' book, nor a 'guide to becoming a successful entrepreneur.' It is rather a thoughtful look, through historical lenses, at a human agent of central importance in economics. We are concerned that a vital concept of economic action remains outside the ebb and flow of most theoretical economics, despite two centuries of formal, historical development. We therefore hope that this book will challenge economic theoreticians to seek and find a way to bring the entrepreneur into the mainstream of economic theory.

Substantial changes have been made in this second edition. The text was enlarged by approximately one third. Two new chapters were added, one which treats U.S. economic thought on the entrepreneur separately (Chapter 7), the other which explores the relationship between the entrepreneur and the firm (Chapter 10). Chapter 4 was expanded to include the ideas of Destutt de Tracy and Henri Saint-Simon. Chapters 5, 6, 7, and 8 contain a more detailed treatment of John Stuart Mill, Alfred Marshall, Léon Walras, Herbert Davenport and Joseph Schumpeter, respectively.

As with all endeavors of this kind, we relied upon the generosity and skill of others in preparing this revision. For their independent, published reviews of the first edition, both pro and con, we would like to thank Professors Reuven Brenner, Israel Kirzner, Brian Hindley, Albro Martin, and E. G. West. Their comments and criticisms helped us to rethink and reorient parts of the original manuscript. Donald Boudreaux, Bruce Caldwell, and Robert Ekelund generously gave of their time and talent to read drafts of the manuscript and provided many helpful suggestions for which we are most grateful. Various editors at Praeger were helpful and encouraging, particularly John Lambert, Michael Fisher, and James Dunton. As always, the patience and quiet support of our wives and families made the task easier than it otherwise would have been.

PREFACE TO THE
FIRST EDITION

This book is a concerted effort to explore the relationship between entrepreneurship and economic activity. It is hoped that it will provide the conceptual framework, basic facts, and historical perspective essential to a better understanding of a highly important subject. Obviously, this slim volume cannot possibly treat such a complex topic in a comprehensive way. But the basic difficulty is not one of space; it is, rather, our still limited and imperfect grasp of a complicated human activity that recently was described by S. M. Kanbur as "the phenomenon which is most emphasized yet least understood by economists."

There is no surfeit of books and articles written on the nature and role of the entrepreneur in society. To date, however, the tendency has been to write historical case studies of individual "captains of industry" or to defend particular theories of entrepreneurial activity. The result is a lack of any singular notion of just who the entrepreneur is and what he does that makes him vital to the economic process. This book takes a different tack by presenting an intellectual history of the subject. By reviewing and examining what past and

PREFACE TO THE FIRST EDITION

present minds have thought about entrepreneurs and entrepreneurship, we hope to build an interpretive framework that will help clarify and augment understanding of this elusive but critical notion in economic theory and practice.

We wish to thank a number of people whose efforts contributed to the conception and completion of this volume. Editor John Lambert of Praeger Publishers has been encouraging and cooperative from the outset. Professor William Breit of the University of Virginia expressed an early vote of confidence in the project and so fueled much of our enthusiasm to undertake it. Professor G. L. S. Shackle, who needs no introduction to the readers of this book, graciously and enthusiastically consented to write the foreword. He also followed the manuscript with interest, offering valuable suggestions and encouragement in the latter stages of its preparation. Bess Yellen and Delores Nuñez of the Manuscript Preparation Center in the School of Business at Auburn University provided peerless typing and editorial assistance with their usual quiet grace and efficiency. Some of the library research for the early chapters was provided by Katherine Graves, a graduate student in the Department of Economics at Auburn University. Our colleagues, Jürgen Backhaus and Roger Garrison, gave generously of their time to read parts of the manuscript, and each offered helpful comments and criticisms. Throughout it all, our wives offered the kind of firm support that made the whole task easier than it otherwise would have been. To all these people we are extremely grateful.

1   *THE PLACE OF THE ENTREPRENEUR IN ECONOMICS*

> The central idea of economics, even when its foundations alone
> are under discussion, must be that of living force and movement.
> Alfred Marshall

The theme of this book is the entrepreneur—his or her defining characteristics and place in the economic order of things. We take it as axiomatic that the entrepreneur is a human agent, and in some measure essential to the economic process. But just who is the entrepreneur?

At the outset, it appears that there are two alternative ways to approach this theme. One is to ask what it is in the human condition, and particularly in the essential nature of business, that gives scope to a person possessing some special combination of talents, and what those talents are. Can a new business venture be imagined, designed in regard to its product and market, its technology and sources of finance, its organization, special knowledge and skills, by any individual chosen at random? Is innovation (in the broadest sense) the province of every human agent? It would seem not. The complex, exacting, and hazardous exploitation of conceived possibilities and seized opportunities requires an exceptional individual. If we elect to call this individual an entrepreneur, the program for defining that term presents itself almost ready-made.

The other approach, the one we have chosen, is to examine the historical literature on the subject to see what meaning has been given to the term entrepreneur in the course of devising theories to deal with other questions and aspects of the economic world. By this second approach, we have herein brought together, with commentary, interpretation, and occasional criticism, the thoughts of many minds on the meaning and significance of entrepreneurship. This chapter sets the stage for what follows.

THE ENTREPRENEUR: CATCHWORD OR CRUCIAL CONCEPT?

The terms *entrepreneur* and *entrepreneurship* are common to the vocabularies of most people today, and the topic occupies a prominent position on the research agendas of scholars from a variety of disciplines including anthropology, history, management, psychology, sociology, and economics. Academic courses in entrepreneurship are now found at undergraduate and graduate levels in many business schools. Centers for the study of entrepreneurship currently operate on many university campuses, and endowed chairs have sprung up across the land to teach this important topic to an eager assortment of future executives.

Entrepreneurship usually has a special meaning in this context. An entrepreneur is identified as a risk taker, a creative venturer into a new business or the one who revives an existing business. Steven Jobs (Apple Computers) and Donald Burrs (People Express) exemplify such persons. According to sociological and psycho-management research, such people are usually first-born children, generally male, college-educated, in their thirties at the time of their first significant venture, highly motivated, creative, energetic, and willing to accept risk (Hisrich 1986). Provided they succeed, such individuals enjoy a "mythical status in America. Symbols of individualism, drive, and intuition, they are the embodiment of our romantic view of capitalism" (Ehrlich 1986, p. 33). In the words of Gumpert, entrepreneurship "is the stuff of which American heros are made" (1986, p. 32).

Since neither entrepreneurs nor entrepreneurship are new concepts in the recorded expanse of human history, it is legitimate to ask: Why this newfound popularization, even idolization, of the entrepreneur? Several explanations are plausible. Each appears to be colored in some measure by the fact that the U.S. economy, like the economies of most industrialized nations, seems to have entered a period of secular decline. The average annual rate of labor productivity growth in the United States fell from 3.3 percent between 1948 and 1965, to 2.3 percent between 1965 and 1973, and again to 1.2 percent between 1973 and 1978. Current estimates show little, if any improvement since then (Link 1987). There are, of course, many reasons for this persistent slowdown, but corporate management has been the brunt of particularly sharp criticism. Writing in the *Harvard Business Review*, Robert Hayes and William Abernathy gave expression to the current economic malaise.

During the past several years American business has experienced a market deterioration of competitive vigor and a growing unease about its overall economic well being. . . . More troubling still, American managers themselves often admit the charge with, at most, a rhetorical shrug of their shoulders. (1980, pp. 67-68)

At the onset of the 1980s, Burton Klein (1979) decried the decline in productivity and equated it with a deterioration of entrepreneurship. He claimed that the U.S. economy was in the process of changing from a dynamic to a static economy, thereby losing its capacity to generate new technical and organizational alternatives to the status quo. Academics and policymakers have responded to waning productivity growth and increased global competition by calling for a revival of entrepreneurship. Ruben Mettler's argument is typical of many others:

The challenge for managers of large and small companies is to learn how to develop (or buy) technology that is best for their specific purposes, how to control the cost of using it, and how to finance it, all while earning enough profit to continue to invest and compete and grow in world markets on a sustained basis. In short, the challenge is to be an entrepreneur. (1986, p. 518)

The issues at hand are so vital that presidential politics have also been brought to bear. A 1985 report, *State of Small Business: A Report of the President*, found that small business, entrepreneurial enterprises accounted for more than 50 percent of the new employment opportunities in the economy since 1982. President Reagan followed up the same theme in his 1985 address to the nation in which he referred to the present decade as the "Age of the Entrepreneur." The intellectual thrust of supply-side economics, moreover—a Reaganesque theme—is based on removing barriers against and erecting incentives to engage in entrepreneurial activity.

Contemporary writers have been quick to capitalize on the popular mood. A flood of recent books on the entrepreneur testifies to the vibrance of the very entrepreneurial spirit about which is being written. The popular press regularly turns out such provocative titles as *Entrepreneurial Megabucks: The 100 Greatest Entrepreneurs of the Last Twenty-Five Years* (A. David Silver); *Entrepreneuring: The Ten Commandments for Building a Growth Company* (Steven C. Brandt); *Innovation and Entrepreneurship: Practices and Principles* (Peter E. Drucker); *Going For It! How to Succeed as an Entrepreneur* (Victor Kiam).

Popular writers of the day often posit their own definitions and conceptualizations of the entrepreneur. Sometimes these conceptualizations are historically based and sometimes they are not. We would expect that academics and professional economists, who are generally more alert to historical precedent, would follow a different pattern. Yet the historical record on the nature of the entrepreneur is so diverse, it is unclear whether academic practice does in fact differ much from popular practice. This book was written with two objectives in mind: First, to help build a bridge between popular and academic usage; second, to expose the raw materials needed to construct an interpretative framework capable of illuminating the nature of entrepreneurship and its role in economic theory.

IMAGINATION, ENTREPRENEURSHIP, AND THE ECONOMIC PARADIGM

Entrepreneurship implies economic activity, and economics, as Ludwig von Mises informed us, is human action. Therefore two questions confront us immediately: What is it that makes man distinctly human? And, What is that combination of gifts that makes entrepreneurs stand out from the wider population? Both answers have a common root. The first question is problematic, and almost any answer given is likely to be controversial. The late Jacob Bronowski, a highly respected scientist and humanist, found the answer to man's uniqueness in his forward-looking imagination:

There are many gifts that are unique in man; but at the centre of them all, the root from which all knowledge grows, lies the ability to draw conclusions from what we see to what we do not see, to move our minds through space and time, and to recognise ourselves in the past on the steps to the present. (1973, p. 56)

This definition is satisfying in a certain sense, but it nevertheless begs the more fundamental question of what it is in the human condition that gives prominence to this act of forward-looking imagination. A part of the answer to this last query must surely involve the concept of time and the nature of the constraint it places on individual choices. Every decision implies a present commitment to some future course of events. But it is the nature of time that we do not know what the future holds, no matter how much control we exert on the present. This is the sense of G. L. S. Shackle's statement in the Foreword that "in choosing [a] present act we are in the nature of things in some respects blind." We are never completely blind, however. As Shackle also informs us, we have reason and knowledge. On the basis of reason and knowledge we can predict what consequences follow our present choices, but we can never know what they will be. Thus our choices are invariably accompanied by anticipation, which itself is an act of the imagination.

Epistemology, the study of the method and grounds of knowledge, is beyond the limited scope of our subject, but we nevertheless hold the view that regarding the creative process of discovery, the basic entrepreneurial act, there is little difference between the scientist and the businessman/entrepreneur. Apparent differences may exist in the motivation and/or the milieu of each class of actors. But consider the process of discovery alone for the moment. Those geniuses who have been responsible for the major innovations in the history of thought or in the world of affairs seem to have certain characteristics in common. One shared characteristic is skepticism, sometimes carried to the point of iconoclasm, in their attitudes to traditional ideas or ways of doing things. The other is an open-mindedness, often verging on naive credulity, toward new concepts and techniques. Out of this combination comes the capacity to perceive a familiar situation or problem in a new light. As Arthur Koestler (1959) has reminded us, the creative process is a wrenching away of a concept or technique from its traditional context or meaning. Over and over again, history has demonstrated this to be the case. Newton associated the fall of an apple not with its ripeness but with the motion of the moon. Henry Ford saw in the monotony of repetitive tasks the economic advantages of the assembly line and of mass production. The computer punch card had its prototype in the Jacquard loom. And so it has been throughout the history of the creative process.

Is it the function of the entrepreneur to create profit opportunities or merely to react to those opportunities that exist but have not yet been recognized? In the following chapters we shall see that both claims have been advanced. It would seem, however, that both kinds of behavior spring from the same center of imagination in the human psyche. Does it not take an act of forward-looking imagination to recognize a profit opportunity and act on it? Are not the same data received, interpreted, and acted upon differently by different individuals? How can we explain these differences? Are they not merely different powers of imagination?

Because we cannot know the future consequences of our present actions, each of us, as a decision maker, is placed at risk. As Shackle so aptly put it, the entrepreneur is a man whose characteristic act is a gamble on his imagination. Perhaps in this area the entrepreneur is different from the scientist, but if so, the difference is merely one of degree. The scientist usually stakes his chips in the form of his reputation, and in any event, all decisions involve commiting resources that have alternative uses, thereby incurring opportunity costs. Nevertheless, the ensuing historical exegesis will demonstrate that the position of risk in the theory of entrepreneurship is a matter on which past and present writers have shown little inclination to agree.

What, then, are the earmarks of the entrepreneur? What gifts of intellect, imagination, critical judgment, capacity for resolute action and sustained effort, courage, and detachment are required if a person is to bring novelty into the business scene and to shape in some degree its ongoing historical evolution? Is the continual and sometimes dramatic transformation of the means, ends, and methods of business the work of a type of moving spirit, a class of exceptional people? If so, what are they like, what precisely is exceptional in their psyches, their situations in life, their sources of inspiration?

Finally, what sets their thoughts on fire and spurs them to action?

The answers to these questions form an ambitious research agenda that cannot be completed in so short a book as this. But the questions themselves provide a touchstone for the historical survey that follows. In this survey we shall see how the minds that shaped economic thought on the subject of the entrepreneur grappled or failed to come to grips with the questions we have posed. This survey thereby serves two purposes. It helps fill a void in the intellectual ancestry of a subject of vital importance to a dynamic economy, and it demonstrates in a most convincing way that the concept of entreneurship bids fair to the claim of being the most elusive concept within the purview of economics.

By its nature, this study also raises, at least in indirect fashion, the question of what claim the idea of equilibrium has to dominate economists' thoughts and modes of analysis so pervasively. In a business world where dramatic success is so constantly the result of new knowledge, of discovery, invention, innovation, and all the activities that involve imagination, what is the relevance or supporting evidence of the supposition that history leads to a complete and comprehensive mutual adjustment of all rival interests? The purpose of the businessman/entrepreneur is to outwit rivals, to destroy or to swallow them up. Can his or her achievement of purpose be characterized by a general equilibrium, the balancing of all conflicting interests?

Many economists find such questions heretical. Others find them futile, perhaps because the answers do not come easily. But economists would do well to remind themselves that the equilibrium method came to economics through classical mechanics and that the physical principles that regulate the universe have been revised several times since that bygone era. To date few economists have tried to explore the implications for the social order of Boltzmann's entropy law, Heisenberg's uncertainty principle, or Einstein's theory of relativity. Do these principles have their analogs in the social order, as was assumed the case for classical mechanics in an earlier century?

We raise these provocative questions not because we have ready answers to them but because we cannot afford to ignore them indefinitely. The kind of environment in which the successful entrepreneur operates forces such questions upon us, however uncomfortable these questions make us. If the entrepreneur is a major force of change in the economic realm, if he is unique in the gifts he brings to the exercise of his peculiar function, if he deals in the unknowable consequences of his present and past actions, then as economists we should question the dominant mode of analysis that recognizes none of these attributes. Whether our understanding of the nature and significance of the entrepreneur in the social order has been helped or hindered by the dominance of the equilibrium paradigm is an open question. In order to answer that question it would seem necessary to have the historical record laid bare. In a small measure, the remainder of this book is devoted to that end.

2   THE PREHISTORY OF ENTREPRENEURSHIP

To study the entrepreneur is to study . . . the central figure in economics.

A. H. Cole

The function of the entrepreneur is probably as old as the institutions of barter and exchange. Many economists have recognized the pivotal role of the entrepreneur in a market economy. Yet despite his central importance in economic activity, the entrepreneur has been a shadowy and elusive figure in the history of economic theory. Referred to often but rarely ever studied or even carefully defined, the entrepreneur winds his way through economic history, producing results often attributed to faceless institutions or impersonal market structures.

Before research in entrepreneurship can be brought to a mature stage, we must be able to answer two simple yet critical questions: (1) Who is the entrepreneur? and (2) What does he do that makes him unique? Regrettably, the answers to these questions are far from clear-cut. There are almost as many definitions of entrepreneurship as there are students of the subject. This book seeks tentative answers to these questions in the annals of intellectual history. We are not aware of any book-length treatment of the history of entrepreneurship as an element of economic theory. Joseph Schumpeter, in his compendious *History of Economic Analysis* (1954) traces the history of the subject at some length, but there is much of the story that he does not tell. The rest of the intellectual landscape is dotted with smaller monuments to the concept of entrepreneurship in the form of journal articles here and there.

As an independent discipline, economics is hardly more than two centuries old. This makes it an elder statesman among the social sciences but a mere babe in the history of human activity. We must begin our search for understanding of entrepreneurship in the intellectual prehistory of economics, the era before Adam Smith gave form and structure to the subject in 1776. The most striking thing about this early period is the blankness of its record regarding the nature of entrepreneurship.

MERCHANTS AND ADVENTURERS

Early economic thought was sensitive to the fact that economic activity is human activity and that acting agents can roughly be divided into two classes: those who lead and those who follow. Entrepreneurial talent, however ill-defined for the present, has always been closely aligned with the quality of leadership. Aside from royalty, the entrepreneur was typically found among the ranks of merchants or the military. Military leaders especially qualified, because in this period of time, wars were often fought for economic reasons. The general who designed and executed a successful strategy in battle took considerable risks and stood to gain substantial economics benefits.

Ancient merchants also exposed themselves and their

possessions to risk in a way not unlike the military leader. Indeed, in early times the functions of trader and adventurer were often merged in the same individual. Marco Polo, for example, was an adventurer seeking to establish vital trade routes to the Orient, a land of many new and fascinating products. Even less peripatetic merchants were customarily exposed to many risks. Courage in business was not equated with courage in battle, however, and the merchant was held in low esteem by the ancient philosophers. Aristotle, for one, recognized the place of the merchant in society but did not regard him as having a high calling. On the contrary, he must be watched constantly, lest society suffer from his overzealousness and rapaciousness. According to Aristotle,

Of the two sorts of money-making one, . . . is a part of household management, the other is retail trade: the former necessary and honorable, the latter a kind of exchange which is justly censured; for it is unnatural, and a mode by which men gain from one another. (1924, p. 20)

Of course the ancient Greek paranoia over maintenance of the status quo was partly a result of interpreting economic activity as a zero-sum game, an idea whose dominance persisted into the eighteenth century. By zero-sum game we mean a process whereby the gains to any one party or group of individuals are exactly offset by the losses to a second party or group of individuals. Ancient Greek and medieval philosophers tended to think that one person's gain (i.e., profit) was another person's loss, so that trade did nothing to enhance the aggregate well-being of society.

Centuries of experience with markets should have taught us otherwise, but it is remarkable how stubbornly this idea persists in contemporary society. Profit, the return to successful entrepreneurship, remains suspect in the minds of many well-educated people today, partly because of a long Western tradition of equating businessman with bogeyman.

EARLY FORMS OF BUSINESS ORGANIZATION

The tendency to emphasize the importance of human decisions in the strategic nature of economic activity depends to a large extent on the kind of business organization that prevails. In the ancient and medieval worlds, trade took place on a relatively small scale. The link between the capitalist and the merchant adventurer depended on the contract they signed. During the Middle Ages, the most common contract specified a loan by the capitalist to the merchant at the standard rate of 22.5 percent (including insurance). In these arrangements the capitalist was a passive risk bearer, whereas the merchant-adventurer took an active role in trade or commerce.

This type of business contract, known as the *societas maris*, persisted in commercial societies for many centuries. In Venice, Europe's most active trading society in the thirteenth century, the same business organization became formalized in the *colleganza*, a cooperative agreement between a traveling and an investing partner. The terms were less generous to the Venetian entrepreneur than to his foreign counterparts. According to Raymond de Roover (1963a), the traveling partner always embarked on a hazardous sea voyage, handled the actual business, and risked his life and limb, but received only one-fourth of the profits, while the lion's share of three-fourths went to the investing partner. In explanation, de Roover proffered that the capitalist received a higher return because "life was cheap and capital scarce" (1963a, p. 49).

By contrast, Fritz Redlich (1966) found the explanation for high returns to capital in the medieval prohibition against usury. The Church's prohibition enjoined medieval businessmen from borrowing capital in some loan markets and paying a fair rate of interest thereon. But certain kinds of business contracts were exempt from the prohibition, including the colleganza and the societas maris. Thus, entrepreneurs were forced by religious sanction to seek credit in arrangements approved (or at least not forbidden) by the Church. The consequent restriction on the supply of business capital could account for higher interest rates.

Economic writers during the Middle Ages were primarily theologians writing under the auspices of the Church. De Roover (1963b, pp. 82–83) claims that they were interested primarily in deontology. Their consequent preoccupation with ethics seriously limited their interest in certain questions, among them entrepreneurship. Duns Scotus and San Bernardino were exceptions. They agreed that merchants were entitled to compensation for risk and recompense for their labor; however, in amounts limited by "justice." San Bernardino also stressed the qualities good merchants should possess: They must have good judgement with respect to risks, be well-informed with respect to goods qualities, prices and costs, be attentive to detail, and prepared to suffer hardships and all manner of risks.

PROPERTY RIGHTS AND THE ENTREPRENEURIAL FUNCTION

Two main points can be gleaned from a review of ancient and medieval literature on entrepreneurship, sparse though it may be. First, the merchant-adventurer was a commonplace of ancient and medieval societies. Second, his success or lack of it depended on how well he fared in overcoming risk and/ or legal and institutional constraints. Much of the remainder of this book deals with the relationship of risk to entrepreneurship. It is therefore incumbent upon us to say something about legal and institutional factors.

Entrepreneurs (whether ancient or modern) work within an institutional environment which itself often yields to entrepreneurial efforts. That is to say, there are "political entrepreneurs" who expend efforts to change institutional structures and practices in order to benefit themselves. While the actions of such participants do not constitute a major concern of this book, it is important to recognize at an early stage of inquiry the vital role of institutions in shaping entrepreneurial activities and rewards. This point is underscored by the following historical example.

An early manifestation of entrepreneurship involving risk bearing and individual initiative existed in the medieval practice of tax farming. A tax farmer is one who successfully bids for the exclusive right to collect taxes in the name of the Crown. The amount of each bid is related in a predictable way to the bidder's evaluation of the amount of taxes he can collect. The advantage to the monarch who farms out the collection of taxes is that he knows his revenues and receives them in advance. The risk to the tax farmer is that he may collect less tax revenue than what he paid for the exclusive right to collect taxes. Of course, if he collects more than the amount of his bid, the difference is his to keep. The practice of tax farming can be traced back as far as ancient Greece and may, upon closer investigation, be found to be even older.

The practice of tax farming helps to explain how property rights ownership and the security of these rights impinge on the behavior of entrepreneurs. The incentive that spurs each entrepreneur to action is the opportunity to obtain profit. But making profit, while a necessary condition, is not a sufficient condition for entrepreneurial activity. The entrepreneur must also be reasonably assured that he may keep entrepreneurial profits that he acquires legitimately. Thus, certain institutional practices in a market economy will tend to encourage a high level of entrepreneurial activity, especially (1) a free and open economy that permits equal access to entrepreneurial opportunities, (2) guarantees of ownership in property legally acquired, and (3) stability of institutional practices that establishes both (1) and (2).

Perhaps the prevalence and longevity of tax farming as an entrepreneurial activity were due to the relatively greater security enjoyed by the fiscal entrepreneur as against the merchant-adventurer whose goods were subject to fire, theft, storm, and other destruction, and whose profit did not always reflect his diligence in supervision or management.

THE EVOLUTION OF A CONCEPT

Redlich maintains that in the model of a business enterprise the provision of capital and management and strategic decision making all "stand on the same level; none can be thought away without distorting reality to the point of no return. On the other hand, when we look at individual enterprises in specific situations any one of these three functions may temporarily become 'primary'" (1966, p. 715). Something analogous can be said about the history of entrepreneurship. Over time, one aspect or another comprising "entrepreneurship" has vied for attention. Historically the risk-bearing function of entrepreneurship became less important after the establishment of limited liability and the new forms of business organization it generated. Subsequently, innovation came to be stressed over other aspects of entrepreneurship in theories of economic development. The third wave of entrepreneurial theories—one which still ripples through modern economic literature—stresses the importance of perception and adjustment in an equilibrating framework.

The term *entrepreneur* does not appear often in the prehistory of economics. It is a word of French origin that first made an obtrusive appearance in the writing of Richard Cantillon, an eighteenth-century businessman and financier whose ideas on the subject are treated in the next chapter. Cantillon is significant in this connection not merely because he used the term but because he infused it with precise economic content and gave it analytic prominence. The fact that common, though imprecise, usage of the term existed prior to Cantillon is corroborated by an entry in Savary's *Dictionnaire Universel de Commerce* (Paris, 1723) in which *entrepreneur* is defined as one who undertakes a project; a manufacturer; a master builder. An earlier form of the word, *entreprendeur*, appears as early as the fourteenth century (Hoselitz 1960). Throughout the sixteenth and seventeenth centuries the most frequent usage of the term connoted a government contractor, usually of military fortifications or public works.

The typical entrepreneur of the Middle Ages, usually a cleric, was "the man in charge of the great architectural works: castles and fortifications, public buildings, abbeys and cathedrals" (Hoselitz 1960, p. 237). Until the end of the twelfth century, the functions of inventor, planner, architect, builder, manager, employer, and supervisor were all combined in the notion of an entrepreneur, but risk bearing and capital provision were not part of the concept. As capitalism began to supplant feudalism, a clearer distinction emerged between the one who performed artistic and technical functions and the one who undertook the commercial aspects of a great task. Cantillon's work is a watershed in the development of entrepreneurial theory precisely because by the time we get to his treatment of the subject, emphasis is being placed squarely on the purely commercial aspects of getting things done in a market economy.

3

FIRST STEPS ON
A NEW PATH

Many people set themselves up ... as merchants or entrepreneurs ... they pay a certain price for produce depending on where they purchase it, to resell wholesale or retail at an uncertain price.

Richard Cantillon

RICHARD CANTILLON

The crucial role of the entrepreneur in economic theory was first and foremost recognized by Richard Cantillon, whose *Essai sur la nature du commerce en général* was published posthumously in 1755, after circulating privately for two decades among a small group of French economists. Although several French writers borrowed freely from Cantillon's manuscript during its private circulation, it was relatively neglected after its publication until William Stanley Jevons rediscovered it in the nineteenth century. Today, Cantillon's *Essai* is rightfully considered a classic of early economic literature. Jevons enthusiastically called it "the cradle of political economy."

The details of Cantillon's life and activities are rather sparse. He was of Irish extraction, and is often confused with a relative of the same name. The exact year of his birth has so far defied identification. He was a successful banker and financier, but several of his business transactions were marked by controversy. In Paris, he made a fortune at the expense of John Law's infamous inflationary scheme known as the "Mississippi Bubble." Demonstrating considerable entrepreneurial skill in his own right, Cantillon anticipated the course of events entrained by Law's "system," and profited handsomely from the financial opportunities which it presented.

In 1716, Law obtained permission from France's prince regent to establish a royal bank. Shortly thereafter he secured an exclusive franchise to form a trading company in the New World that was popularly known as the Mississippi Company. The company monopolized French foreign trade and eventually began to assume the French government's debt by trading shares of the company's stock for certificates of indebtedness. With the certificates came the exclusive right to collect certain taxes. Promises of large dividends to investors pushed share prices up sharply, and a frenzy of stock speculation ensued. The system came crashing down when stock values rose out of proportion to the real value of the company's assets. In 1720, the Mississippi Bubble burst.

Cantillon made a great deal of money by liquidating his Mississippi Company holdings before the speculative boom peaked. With the proceeds of his own shares reinvested in Britain and Holland, he fed the British mania for speculation by advancing funds to English speculators who bought shares in the Mississippi Company that they subsequently pledged as collateral for their loans. Confident of the ultimate failure of Law's scheme, Cantillon sold the collateralized shares before the price of the stock broke, thus pocketing speculative profits in addition to the interest he collected on the loans he made. This practice provoked numerous lawsuits by his borrowers, but Cantillon successfully defended himself against their claims. This display of financial acumen stamped Cantillon as a successful entrepreneur in his own right, but his intellectual legacy was a greater testimony to his talents.

ENTREPRENEURS AND MARKETS

Cantillon's historic *Essai* sketched the outlines of a nascent market economy founded on individual property rights and based on economic interdependency, or what he called mutual "need and necessity." In this early market economy Cantillon recognized three classes of economic agents: (1) landowners, who are financially independent; (2) entrepreneurs, who engage in market exchanges at their own risk in order to make a profit; and (3) hirelings, who eschew active decision making in order to secure contractual guaranties of stable income (i.e., fixed wage contracts).

Cantillon depicts the landowners as the "fashion leaders" in this society. By virtue of their wealth and social status they establish patterns of consumption in conformance with their individual tastes and preferences. It has been said that Cantillon placed the landowner at the top of the economic hierarchy, but a closer examination of his work reveals the *entrepreneur* as the central economic actor.

Cantillon's entrepreneur is someone who engages in exchanges for profit; specifically, he or she is someone who exercises business judgment in the face of uncertainty. This uncertainty (of future sales prices for goods on their way to final consumption) is rather carefully circumscribed. As Cantillon describes it, entrepreneurs buy at a certain price to sell again at an uncertain price, with the difference being their profit or loss.

An important aspect of Cantillon's theory is that it stresses the *function*, not the personality of the entrepreneur. His idea is sweeping in its application, embracing many different occupations and cutting across production, distribution, and exchange. "The farmer," Cantillon (1931, pp. 47–49) wrote, "is an entrepreneur who promises to pay to the landowner, for his farm or land, a fixed sum of money without assurance of the profit he will derive from this enterprise." As an entrepreneur-producer, the farmer decides how to allocate his land among various uses "without being able to foresee which of these will pay best." He must contend with the vagaries of weather and demand, placing himself at risk. Cantillon concludes that no one "can foresee the number of births and deaths of the people in a state in the course of the year," or the rise and decline of family spending, "and yet the price of the farmer's produce depends naturally upon these unforeseen circumstances, and consequently he conducts the enterprise of his farm at an uncertainty."

In a market economy, the farmer is linked to consumers by other economic agents, who also face uncertain incomes. Goods are usually distributed by middlemen, who are intermediaries between producers and consumers. To the extent that these people face uncertainty in the marketplace, they too are entrepreneurs. These middlemen find markets for their services mainly in the cities. Thus, Cantillon (1931, p. 49) observed that more than half of farm output is consumed in the cities, where entrepreneurs set up shop to receive goods from the farms and to resell to ultimate consumers. The carriers and the wholesalers, through whose hands goods pass as they move from the farm to the customer, are also put at risk because of daily price fluctuations in the city. It is almost as though Cantillon were trying to tell his readers that *time* is the handmaiden of uncertainty.

The city creates opportunities for other entrepreneurs who are residents and who are willing to take risks in order to make goods available at the appropriate time and place. Each represents a link in the chain of distribution. Thus entrepreneurs who carry goods to the city usually sell to wholesalers, who subsequently sell at retail to ultimate consumers. In this manner, part of the risk is shifted from carriers to wholesalers and from wholesalers to retailers, each of whom provides time and place utility to consumers.

Cantillon asserted that as markets develop, self-interested entrepreneurs spring up everywhere, goaded on by the lure of profit, and joined together by mutual need, or reciprocity. These entrepreneurs are encouraged because they know that consumers are willing to pay a little extra in order to buy in small quantities, when it is convenient, rather than bear the inconvenience and expense of stockpiling large quantities for their ultimate use (Cantillon 1931, pp. 51–53).

Cantillon's *Essai* contains over a hundred references to the entrepreneur as a pivotal figure in the economic process. He laid it down as a general principle that entrepreneurs conduct all the production, circulation, and exchange in a market economy. As a motive force, entrepreneurs are much more important than the landowners, who collectively determine aggregate demand, but otherwise retire to the sidelines of economic activity.

Cantillon broke with convention in emphasizing the economic function of the entrepreneur over his/her social status. Social standing is practically irrelevant to Cantillon's notion of entrepreneurship. He went so far as to identify even beggars and robbers as entrepreneurs, provided they take chances (i.e., face economic uncertainty). Yet being an entrepreneur does not exclude one from being something else. Entrepreneurs and nonentrepreneurs alike are joined in reciprocal trade agreements with other market participants. Entrepreneurs therefore "become consumers and customers one in regard to the other," and proportion themselves to their customers in accordance with the laws of supply and demand. Like every other market, the market for entrepreneurs will adjust to market exigencies. "If there are too many hatters" Cantillon (1931, p. 53) wrote, "for the number of people who buy hats . . . , some who are least patronized must become bankrupt," whereas, "if they be too few it will be a profitable undertaking which will encourage new hatters to open shops . . . so it is that the entrepreneurs of all kinds adjust themselves to risks in a state."

UNCERTAINTY AND RISK

Cantillon did not provide a detailed analysis of the nature of risk and uncertainty. He took uncertainty for granted as something inherent in the economic activity of the marketplace. He gave the concept of entrepreneurship economic content merely by relating the function of the entrepreneur to uncertainty, and by implication, to risk.

Since the writings of Frank Knight (see Chapter 7), it is customary in economics to distinguish between risk and uncertainty. Knight pointed out that some forms of risk can be mitigated by insurance. To be insurable, there must be a known probability distribution associated with risk, either because of large numbers of individuals exposed to risk or repeated exposures to the same risk by the same individual.

Although we cannot credit Cantillon with this distinction, it is reasonably clear that the concept of uncertainty central to his analysis is not of the insurable kind. In Cantillon's world, not only is the information about the future unknown, it is also for the most part, unknowable. While insurance companies tend to underwrite losses from named perils that are calculated to occur with predictable frequency, they do not typically insure against errors in judgement. Yet Cantillon's entrepreneurs are constantly called upon to exercise their business judgement, and if they guess wrong, they must pay the price.

An astute businessman, Cantillon was obviously aware of institutional arrangements that could be invoked to limit risk. But these things were of little consequence to his theory of entrepreneurship. His discussion of uncertainty is cast in the sense of things unknowable. This kind of uncertainty, which we now call "Knightian uncertainty" is inherent in the nature of competitive (rivalrous) market activity, so there is literally no way to separate the concepts of competition and entrepreneurship in Cantillon's vision of the economy. One is a consequence of the other.

CAPITAL AND ENTREPRENEURSHIP

One of the perpetual points of contention in competing theories of entrepreneurship is to what extent the roles of entrepreneur and capitalist can be separated. Specifically, does a risk-bearing theory of entrepreneurship require that an entrepreneur own certain capital assets that are staked in the profit/loss game? More to the point, if one has nothing to lose, then there can be no such thing as a loss. A theory of entrepreneurship that explains economic gains but not economic losses is patently one-sided. On the other hand, if the capitalist and the entrepreneur are one and the same, then economics cannot offer a framework for identifying the return to each function.

On this issue, Cantillon was more expansive than many later writers who took up the same subject. It is clear that Cantillon's entrepreneur must risk something, but it need not be capital in the pecuniary sense. He seemed to appreciate the modern concept of human capital, even though he did not actually formulate the notion. He identified "entrepreneurs of their own labor who need no capital to establish themselves," (1931, p. 53) using examples from commerce (chimney sweeps, water carriers), from art (painters), and from science (physicians, lawyers). He even included beggars and robbers as entrepreneurs.

In order to bring Cantillon's theory up to contemporary standards we must recognize that even the penniless entrepreneur incurs potential losses to the extent that he faces opportunity costs for his time and talents. This issue has been clarified recently by S. M. Kanbur (1980). Consider an individual with no means of his own. Suppose he foresees an opportunity that promises an uncertain rate of return, and he borrows capital at a fixed, contractual rate of interest. If the enterprise does so badly that the borrower cannot repay the contracted amount of principle and interest, the financial loss falls solely on the lender. But as Kanbur argues,

Surely the gains and losses, and hence risks, are to be thought of as being relative to the opportunity cost of the enterprise. For example, it could be that the prospective entrepreneur has open to him a safe return in an alternative occupation. *Relative* to this return, the contract above does indeed present our entrepreneur with the possibility of losses—he *could* end up worse than if he had taken up a safe occupation, though of course he will always end up better than if he had taken up no occupation at all. This is the sense in which the prospective entrepreneur faces risks. . . . (1980, p. 493)

For the man of means who foresees and acts on an uncertain opportunity, the problem remains how to separate his risk-bearing role as capitalist from his risk-bearing role as entrepreneur. Conceptually, it is possible to do this, but we must look to the colleganza of thirteenth-century Venice or the societas maris of ancient Greece for a working model. In these arrangements the functions of capitalist and entrepreneur were separate; the former was an investing partner and the latter a traveling/managing partner. It should be expected that the opportunity cost of the capital in such an arrangement will be different from the opportunity cost of the entrepreneurial effort, and it is in proportion to these different costs that the respective risks have to be conceptualized and, ultimately, measured.

A HARBINGER OF THE FUTURE

Cantillon argued that the origin of entrepreneurship lies in the lack of perfect foresight individuals have with regard to the future. He did not, however, consider this lack of foresight a defect of the market system, rather he accepted it as part of the human condition. Uncertainty is a pervasive fact of everyday life, and those who must deal with it continually in their economic decisions are entrepreneurs. Consequently it is the *function* of the entrepreneur, not his/her personality, that counts for economic analysis. Cantillon was quite emphatic that this function lies at the very heart of a market system, and that without it, the market as we know it, does not operate.

Some other aspects of Cantillon's conception are worth collecting here. His portrayal of the entrepreneur's role in a market economy has a distinct supply-side emphasis. His entrepreneur does not create demand through new production or merchandising techniques. Rather he/she follows the dictates of a class of fashion leaders (the landlords). The entrepreneur thus provides appropriate goods or services at the right time and place in order to satisfy preordained consumer wants. To be effective, he/she must be forward-looking. He/she must be alert, for when particular supplies and demands do not match, the theory calls for the entrepreneur to spring into action. But Cantillon's entrepreneur is not required to be innovative in the strict sense of the term.

The kind of action that engages the entrepreneur's effort is not limited to production, moreover. This is clear from the above passages about middlemen and retailers, as well as from Cantillon's recognition of the arbitrageur as an entrepreneur. Noting the opportunities for profit created by price differences between the countryside and Paris, Cantillon (1931, pp. 150–52) asserted that as long as they can cover transportation costs, entrepreneurs "will buy at a low price the products of the villages and will transport them to the Capital to be sold there at a higher price."

Even a pure arbitrage action such as this involves some uncertainty on the entrepreneur's part. The arbitrageur can perceive that a product sells for one price at one place and at a higher price somewhere else; but if he buys in the first to sell in the second, he must be careful. The transactions are not instantaneous, and something might occur in the interim to change seemingly certain profits into losses.

Although we cannot attribute to Cantillon—nor to any early economist—a full-blown theory of profit, it is noteworthy that he recognized the legitimacy (and necessity) of entrepreneurial profits in order that the function of the entrepreneur be carried out. Thus he established the economic and social necessity of profit early in the history of economic theory.

We believe that Cantillon's conception of the entrepreneur is extremely important to a proper understanding of the concept in economic analysis. But his view did not predominate, nor was it complete in itself. It was myopic in one important respect. Cantillon excluded the "Prince," the landlords, and certain laborers from uncertainty. Today we recognize that economic uncertainty is more pervasive than he allowed. Mises was correct when he asserted that "no proprietor of any means of production, whether they are represented in tangible goods or in money, remains untouched by the uncertainty of the future" (1949, p. 253). Cantillon's notion of entrepreneurship needed to be widened, and at a much later date it was, by Knight and by Ludwig von Mises. But that is another story which will follow in due course.

4   A FORK IN THE ROAD

[The entrepreneur] estimates needs and above all the means to satisfy them.

                                                                    J. B. Say

Cantillon began an important analytical tradition in his adopted country of France. Based on the idea of a circular flow of income, he propounded a vision of how a capitalist economy works, giving pride of place to the entrepreneur. Due to his influence, eighteenth- and nineteenth-century French economists, unlike their British counterparts (at least from Smith to Mill), never lost sight of the pivotal nature and importance of the entrepreneur. The full flowering of the concept, however, was neither rapid nor direct.

After Cantillon's death, economic analysis in France was dominated by a group of writers who called themselves, simply, "The Economists." As that term became more general in its use, however, historians began to refer to this particular group of French writers as "The Physiocrats" (the term *physiocracy* means rule of nature). It was a singular group with a singular leader, François Quesnay. Quesnay shared Cantillon's basic economic vision, and he elaborated Cantillon's notion of the circular-flow of wealth by developing an explicit analytical model, the *Tableau Économique.* It was the first mathematical formulation of a general equilibrium system.

FRANÇOIS QUESNAY

Quesnay entered economics in his sixties, after enjoying considerable success as a physician and author of books on medicine, biology, and philosophy. His renown as a physician brought him to the court of Louis XV, where he personally attended Madame du Pompadour. In economics, his fame rests on his pioneer contributions to national income analysis and his acknowledged leadership of the first cohesive school of economic thought. Quesnay's ability to attract adherents to his views stemmed in part from his magnetic personality and in part from the substance of his analysis. That analysis was rich in theoretic and policy implications, but its full import is not at issue here. What concerns us are the contributions of physiocracy to the theory of entrepreneurship.

Quesnay and his band of disciples analyzed the nature and operation of agrarian capitalism. Their analytic system features three economic classes, which can be distinguished from each other by their respective economic functions. A proprietary class owns property rights in the land that it leases to the productive class (i.e., farmers), who in turn produce the raw materials demanded by a third class, the artisans. The unique feature of physiocratic analysis is that it holds agriculture alone capable of producing a net product, or economic surplus. This surplus is measured by the value of agricultural output over its costs, and is claimed by the proprietors in the form of rent, annually paid to the owners of land.

The merit of Quesnay's analysis is that it underscores the vital importance of capital to economic growth. In the physiocratic system, capital comes from the landlords, who are best positioned to accumulate wealth. Entrepreneurs are present in the economy as farmers. Quesnay distinguished between small-scale farmers (*petite culture*) and large-scale farming (*grande culture*), depicting the entrepreneur as the operator of a large farm. He described the rich farmer as an entrepreneur, "who manages and makes his business profitable by his intelligence and his wealth" (1888, pp. 218–19). Quesnay had in mind a capitalist farmer who owns and manages his business on land owned by another. Thus, his entrepreneur is the independent owner of a business.

Quesnay's emphasis on individual energy, intelligence, and wealth is suggestive, but he did not develop the idea of the entrepreneur further, nor did he extend its application beyond agriculture. In general, Physiocracy ignored the notion of the entrepreneur as a leader of *industry*. Because they considered manufacturing incapable of yielding a surplus, the Physiocrats termed it "sterile" and ranked it subservient to agriculture.

NICOLAS BAUDEAU

Among Quesnay's disciples, one writer in particular developed a theory of entrepreneurship that foreshadowed future developments. He was a clergyman, the Abbé Nicolas Baudeau (1730–1792), who began as a foe of physiocracy but later converted to Quesnay's sect. Baudeau treated the agricultural entrepreneur as a risk bearer, in the manner of Cantillon, but he added a distinctly modern twist. He made the entrepreneur an innovator as well, one who invents and applies new techniques or ideas in order to reduce his costs and thereby raise his profit. These new aspects of entrepreneurship, invention and innovation, represent an important advance over Cantillon's theory because they anticipate the most prominent twentieth-century formulation of entrepreneurship, Joseph Schumpeter's theory of "creative destruction" (see Chapter 8).

Baudeau's notion of entrepreneurship paralleled Cantillon's, but only to a point. Consider the nature of risk faced by the agricultural entrepreneur. The rent he pays to the landlord is the surplus of farm revenue over necessary costs of production, including some payment for his own services. For the tenant farmer, rent is a cost determined in advance of production. The Physiocrats favored stabilizing these costs as much as possible through long-term leases, while wage rates were usually fixed at or near subsistence levels. Thus, the farmer operating with a long-term lease faced certain fixed costs, but uncertain harvests and hence uncertain sales prices. This is precisely the situation of Cantillon's entrepreneur, as we have seen.

The area in which Baudeau went beyond Cantillon was in emphasizing and analyzing the significance of ability. Baudeau underscored the importance of "intelligence," the entrepreneur's ability to collect and process knowledge and information. Intelligence—knowledge and the ability to act—also gives the entrepreneur a measure of control, so that he is not a mere pawn to the capitalist. Baudeau paints the entrepreneur as an active agent: "Such is the goal of the grand productive enterprises; first to increase the harvest by two, three, four, ten times if possible; secondly to reduce the amount of labor employed and so reduce costs by a half, a third, a fourth, or a tenth, whatever possible" (1910, p. 46).

Physiocratic writings are replete with proposals to improve agricultural techniques, many of which were oriented toward the upgrading of human capital or the dissemination of better information. Hoselitz (1960, pp. 246–47) listed several of their proposals: translation of English texts on agriculture; nationwide distribution of handbooks and guides describing new tools, crops, or procedures; prizes; honors; agricultural research; model farms and pilot programs. The Physiocrats were convinced that when the right knowledge became available, profit opportunities would induce desirable innovations. The entrepreneur as innovator thus appeared relatively early in economic literature.

Baudeau's theory of entrepreneurship presupposes that economic events fall into two categories, those that are subject to human control and those that are not. To the extent that the entrepreneur confronts events under his control, his success depends upon knowledge and ability. To the extent that he confronts events beyond his control, he places himself at risk. In this sense, Baudeau's theory of entrepreneurship is more general than Cantillon's, which concentrated on the effects of uncertainty without reference to administrative control.

ANNE-ROBERT JACQUES TURGOT

A.-R. J. Turgot's place in history is assured by his distinguished administrative career in French government, culminating in his service from 1774 to 1776 as finance minister to Louis XVI. Born to a Norman family of ancient nobility, Turgot (1727–1781) was a gifted and precocious young man whose interests ranged over many areas. One of his many gifts was lucid exposition in the field of economics, and although he resisted the label of economist (Meek 1973), his chief accomplishment as a writer was in mapping out the theory of an entrepreneurial economy.

Turgot's ideas did not coincide at all points with those of physiocracy. He was, however, on good terms with the members of Quesnay's inner circle, and he extended the theory of entrepreneurship by establishing the ownership of capital as a separate economic function in business. Turgot's capitalist must decide whether to loan his capital to someone else or to invest it in a business enterprise of his own. If he chooses the latter, he must further choose land, manufacturing, or commerce as a form of investment. If he purchases land, then he becomes both landowner and capitalist. If he invests in various kinds of goods required for his particular business, he becomes an entrepreneur as well as a capitalist. And if he decides to lend his funds in the form of money, he remains a capitalist only. Unlike Cantillon, Turgot did not anticipate the notion of a "pure" entrepreneur.

In Turgot's scheme of things, the ownership of capital is a qualification for becoming an entrepreneur but the two functions are nevertheless distinct. One can be a capitalist without being an entrepreneur, but one cannot be an entrepreneur without also being a capitalist. The distinguishing feature of Turgot's entrepreneur, therefore, is not his capital but his labor. "The capitalist who has become an entrepreneur, in agriculture or industry, is no more of the disposable class [i.e., independent] either as regards himself or his profits, than the mere workmen in those two classes; they are both set aside for the carrying on of their enterprises" (1977, p. 91).

We therefore have, in Turgot, a theory of the entrepreneur who is a capitalist but who looks to his own labor for his distinctive return. This is emphasized by the following statement from Turgot:

[M]oney employed in agriculture, in industry or in commerce, ought to produce a more considerable profit than the revenue of the same capital employed in the purchase of estates, or the interest of money placed on loan; for since these employments require, in addition to the capital advanced, much care and labor, if they were not more lucrative, it would be more advantageous to secure an equal revenue which might be enjoyed without having to do anything. It is necessary then, that, besides the interest of his capital, the entrepreneur should draw every year a profit to recompense him for his care, his labor, his talents and his risks, and to furnish him in addition that which he may replace the annual wear and tear of his advances, which he is obliged from the very first to convert into effects which are liable to deterioration and which are, moreover, exposed to all kinds of accidents (1977, p. 86).

Ronald Meek (1973) has argued that Cantillon analyzed a society in which the capitalist-entrepreneur was just beginning to separate himself from the ranks of independent workmen, whereas Turgot analyzed an economy in which this process had been completed, and in which the capitalist system had consolidated itself in all fields of economic activity. In his

Reflections on the Formation and Distribution of Wealth (1766), Turgot painted a clear picture of an economy in which capitalism embraces all spheres of production. In his view, the "industrious" classes are divided into entrepreneurs and hired workers. Turgot insisted on a sharp, but somewhat artificial, differentiation between the profit of the former and the wage of the latter. He also maintained that free competition is widespread and monopoly nonexistent; that land-ownership is merely another kind of investment in capital; and that a general glut of goods is impossible because savings are transformed immediately into investment. He did not incorporate into his theory any built-in specification about technological progress, nor any hint that the entrepreneur is an innovator (or anything more than a capitalist-laborer), nor did he emphasize the dynamic aspects of the economy.

It is instructive to compare Turgot's representation of the entrepreneur with Quesnay's and Baudeau's. Although Quesnay did not elaborate a complete theory of entrepreneurship, his portrayal of the entrepreneur as a farmer who produces value by "his intelligence and his wealth" contains an abundance of hidden meaning that subsequently provided a point of departure for both Baudeau and Turgot. Baudeau added elements of organization, innovation, and risk. Turgot ignored innovation, but stressed supervision, and generalized the entrepreneurial function to all sectors of the economy. Hoselitz (1960) placed Turgot's theory of entrepreneurship midway between the early French view, which holds the entrepreneur to be chiefly a risk bearer (e.g., Cantillon and to some extent Baudeau), or a coordinator of production (e.g., Say and to some extent Baudeau), and the English view, which saw the entrepreneur chiefly as a capitalist.

JEAN-BAPTISTE SAY

Continuing a French tradition inaugurated by Cantillon, J. B. Say (1767–1832) made the entrepreneur the pivot of the entire process of production and distribution. Hoselitz (1960) claims that Say's inspiration and strong views on the subject came from his practical experience as an industrial entrepreneur (he managed a textile mill in Pas-de-Calais), rather than from his acquaintance with other French economists. Nevertheless, Say embellished a concept of the entrepreneur that was fundamentally Turgot's—minus the common link to the capitalist.

Say developed his treatment of entrepreneurship most fully in the later editions of his *Traité d'économie politique* (1st ed., 1803) and in his *Cours complet d'économie politique pratique* (1st ed., 1828–29). His analysis proceeds on two different levels. On the one hand, he employed empirical descriptions of what entrepreneurs in his day actually did under existing institutional constraints. On the other hand, he exposed and analyzed the central function of the entrepreneur independently of any particular social framework. In this last effort Say moved toward a general theory of entrepreneurship.

The difference in these two treatments of the subject is more a matter of scientific method than is first apparent. According to Hoselitz,

The actual behavior patterns of entrepreneurs, their motives and objectives may display a considerable degree of variation, both as between persons or industries, as well as between countries and geographical areas. The task of developing a theory of entrepreneurship consists in selecting those aspects of entrepreneurial behavior which are most significant and in determining the degree of generality with which they are found. In other words out of the manifold and different acts which entrepreneurs have performed or may be expected to perform one has to eliminate all those which are "accidental" or which are the result of special circumstances of the person, the time, the locality, the industry, or other factors. Those acts which are left constitute then the most typical forms of entrepreneurial behavior and we can then indicate how commonly they are found. This procedure results not only in an entrepreneurial theory, but indicates at the same time whether, and to what extent entrepreneurial activity is dependent upon certain institutional relations. (1960, p. 252)

As we asserted in Chapter 2, the vigor of entrepreneurial activity depends upon the composition, distribution, and security of property rights. Because entrepreneurial activity is profit seeking, it requires incentives to propel it. These incentives are provided by the structure of property rights within a representative government. Say was quite clear on this, avowing that "political economy recognizes the right of property solely as the most powerful of all encouragements to the multiplication of wealth." Furthermore, where private property exists in reality as well as in right, "then, and then only, can the sources of production, namely land, capital, and industry, attain their utmost degree of fecundity" (1845, p. 127).

Say's theory of the entrepreneur is part of a threefold division of human industry into distinct operations. The first step is the scientific one. Before any product can be made, say a bicycle, certain knowledge about the nature and purpose of it must be understood. It must be known, for example, that a wheel is capable of continuous, circular motion and that a force exerted on a chain and sprockets can propel the wheel forward. The second step, the entrepreneurial one, is the application of this knowledge to a useful purpose (i.e., the development of a mechanism—the bicycle) with one or more wheels capable of transporting someone from one place to another. The final step, the productive one, is the manufacture of the item at the hands of manual labor.

Say's entrepreneur performs a social function, even though Say does not make him a member of a distinct social class. He is a principal agent of production, whose role is vital to the production of utility. His applications of knowledge must not be mere random events. They must meet a "market" test, that is, in order to be entrepreneurial, each application must lead to the creation of value or utility. This requires sound judgment, one of the key characteristics of Say's entrepreneur. Say emphasized this feature in a number of ways. In his *Treatise* he observed that the entrepreneur

estimates needs and above all the means to satisfy them, . . . [and] compares the end with these means. Hence his principal quality is to have good judgment. He can lack the personal knowledge of science, by judiciously employing that of others, he can avoid dirtying his own hands by using the hands of others, but he must not lack judgment; for then he might produce at great expense something which has no value. (1840, vol. 1, p. 100)

Say's entrepreneur is an economic catalyst, a pivotal figure. But Say did not follow Cantillon, by making uncertainty the mainstay of entrepreneurship. Risk is incidental to Say's notion of entrepreneurship because he saw no necessary dependency of entrepreneurial activity upon capital accumulation. For the first time in economic literature, entrepreneurial activity became virtually synonymous with management, in the contemporary sense of that term. Management may, but does not necessarily, supply capital to the enterprise. And Say had no difficulty, theoretically speaking, separating the entrepreneurial function from the capitalist function, even though both functions could be, and often were, combined in the same person.

In the final analysis, Say's entrepreneur is a superintendent and an administrator. Emphasizing the combination of talents required of the successful entrepreneur, Say declared:

[The entrepreneur] requires a combination of moral qualities, that are not often found together. Judgment, perseverance, and a knowledge of the world, as well as of business. He is called upon to estimate, with tolerable accuracy, the importance of the specific product, the probable amount of the demand, and the means of its production: at one time he must employ a great number of hands; at another, buy or order the raw material, collect laborers, find consumers, and give at all times a rigid attention to order and economy; in a word, he must possess the art of superintendence and administration. (1845, pp. 330-31)

Hoselitz (1960) drew two lines of distinction between Say and Cantillon, both of which are questionable. One distinction is that Say's entrepreneur is a universal mediator (e.g., between landlord and capitalist; between scientist and laborers; between producers and consumers, etc.), whereas Cantillon's entrepreneur is not. This claim is dubious because Say makes no allowance for the most active of mediators, the arbitrageur, whereas Cantillon points explicitly to the arbitrageur as an entrepreneur. Moreover, Cantillon gives the entrepreneur the sole function of mediating discrepancies between quantities demanded and quantities supplied in a market economy. By sheer frequency of reference in the *Essai*, the entrepreneur is virtually everywhere in this capacity.

Hoselitz claims a second distinction insofar as Say's entrepreneur, unlike Cantillon's and the Physiocrats', is not confined to a capitalist society. Technically, this is correct, but Say's arguments in general were calculated to reaffirm the desirable social consequences of individual self-interest, and he was fully aware (as was Adam Smith) that the social framework that permitted the full flowering of self-interest was that of the market economy. On a lesser point, however, Hoselitz is quite correct: Say's entrepreneur (mediator) may appear in a primitive society before capital has been accumulated. In other words, the entrepreneur could direct and supervise raw materials and manual labor without the application of capital. (But surely the same holds for Cantillon's beggar and robber "entrepreneurs".)

One aspect of Say's theory is particularly important because it sets the terms of the traditional paradigm and also provides a point of departure for future breaks with tradition. Say's entrepreneur may be characterized as a "guardian" of equilibrium. The "judgment" extolled by Say as a requisite of entrepreneurial activity is confined to relations *within* a production process and does not extend beyond that process to the discovery of new processes or to changes inspired by a new social structure. Because he did not see a necessary relationship between capital accumulation (investment) and entrepreneurial activity, Say did not place the entrepreneur in a dynamic environment. His role was conceived within a purely stationary equilibrium characterized by the equality of prices of products with their costs of production. The primary source of entrepreneurial income in this system is not profit as a premium for risk but rather wages as a payment for a highly skilled type of scarce labor.

In later works, Say (1845) did portray the entrepreneur as a kind of superior laborer. He extended the analogy to include a kind of "market" for entrepreneurs, in which their wages were determined by supply and demand, and he went to some length in discussing the determinants of entrepreneurial supply. From a narrow theoretic standpoint, his treatment of the entrepreneur was a step forward because it distinguished between the respective contributions in production of human and nonhuman agents. But it did not move the concept any closer to a "pure" theory of entrepreneurship.[1]

By portraying the entrepreneur chiefly as a superior form of labor, Say consciously or unconsciously directed attention away from the uniqueness of the entrepreneur and thus from his/her role as a force of change in a dynamic economy.

DESTUTT DE TRACY AND HENRI SAINT-SIMON

Say was a dominant influence on nineteenth-century French economics. Like Smith, he was able to capture the spirit of his times, and the organizational schema of his *Treatise* proved to be much more amenable to the pedagogy of economics, which was becoming commonplace among institutions of higher learning. It therefore became a major "textbook" at universities on both sides of the Atlantic, particularly in America, where its adoption was widespread. New entrants in the competition for ideas soon appeared, however. Among the many, two are especially prominent—one for its clarity, the other for its prophecy.

A. L. C. Destutt de Tracy (1754–1836) and Henri de Saint-Simon (1760–1825) shared the advantage of noble birth at a time when the rank and privileges of nobility in France were threatened on all sides. Strictly speaking, neither was an economist, although both confronted social issues that could not be extricated from economic considerations.

Tracy was one of the last *philosophes* and along with Say, one of the earliest members of the French liberal school. He coined the term *ideology*, by which he meant the science of ideas. Only later did the term take on a pejorative sense, primarily because of Marx. There is no subject in economics to which he contributed greatly, but he nevertheless had a remarkable ability to attract great minds. Tracy rejected the physiocratic notion of value, substituting in its place a labor theory which was subsequently endorsed by David Ricardo. Thomas Jefferson, a great admirer of the French in many things, translated Tracy's *Treatise on Political Economy* into English for an American audience. Furthermore, Jefferson was influenced by Tracy to the point of including "ideology" among the ten projected departments in his plan for the University of Virginia.

Like the Physiocrats, Tracy extolled the virtues of an agricultural economy. But he looked beyond the narrow limits of agriculture and gleaned the essence of a nascent capitalism that was far more pervasive. He was struck first and foremost by the prevalence of economic activities. "The whole of society," he wrote, "is but a continual succession of exchanges;" consequently, "we are all more or less commercial. Commerce and society are one and the same thing" (Tracy 1817, pp. 36, 67). In this formulation of society, Tracy gave the entrepreneur wide berth. "Capital precedes all enterprise, large or small," he asserted, so the enterpriser must have capital to carry out his function. But are the entrepreneur and the capitalist necessarily the same? Tracy answers unequivocally in the affirmative, revealing traces of influence from Say and Turgot:

Theory is the part of the scientific, application that of the undertaker, and execution that of the workman. . . . [T] he man of science and the workman, will always be in the pay of the undertaker. Thus decrees the nature of things; for it is not sufficient to know how to aid an enterprise with the head or the hands: there must be first an enterprise; and he who undertakes it, is necessarily the person who chooses, employs, and pays those who co-operate. Now who is he who can undertake it? It is the man who has already funds, with which he can meet the first expenses of establishment and supplies, and pay wages till the moment of the first returns (1817, pp. 36, 39-40).

Like Cantillon, Tracy underscored the incertitude of the entrepreneur's reward. He recognized risk and opportunity costs as factors affecting the supply of entrepreneurship, but he based the success or failure of the entrepreneur "solely on the quantity of utility he has been able to produce, on the necessity that others are under of procuring it, and . . . on the means they have of paying him for it."

Like Say (Euzent and Martin 1984), Tracy elaborated the nature of public and private interests in a market economy, and the accompanying tendency of "political entrepreneurs" to use the government to their advantage:

In this simple exposition, you already find all the mechanism and the secret springs of that part of production which consists in fabrication. You even discover the germ of opposite interests, which are established between the entrepreneur and those on wages on the one hand, and between the entrepreneur and the consumers on the other, amongst those on wages, between themselves, amongst entrepreneurs of the same kind, even amongst entrepreneurs of different kinds, since it is amongst all these that the means of the mass of consumers are more or less equally divided; and finally amongst consumers themselves, since it is also amongst all of them, that the enjoyment of all the utility produced is divided. You perceive that the hirelings wish there should be few to be hired, and many entrepreneurs, and the entrepreneurs that there should be few entrepreneurs, particularly in the same line as themselves, but many hirelings and also many consumers; and that the consumers, on the contrary, wish for many entrepreneurs and hirelings, and if possible few consumers, for every one fears competition in his own way, and would wish to be alone in order to be master. *If you pursue further the complication of these different interests, in the progress of society, and the action of the passions which they produce, you will soon see all these men implore the assistance of force in favor of the idea with which they are prepossessed; or, at least, under different pretexts, provoke prohibitive laws, to constrain those who obstruct them in this universal contention.* (1817, pp. 41–42, emphasis added)

Claude Henri de Rouvroy, Comte de Saint-Simon, was a pixilated figure in a period that abounded in colorful characters. He is usually not taken seriously by economists because his doctrine is believed to contain elements of socialism and ultimately, mysticism. He was a prolific writer and visionary, who indiscriminately mixed nonsense with clairvoyant prophecy. Above all else, he was obsessed with the nature of social and economic change. His interest in economics sprang from his zeal to rationalize the social order.

Saint-Simon believed that social policy should be adapted to the needs of production. He welcomed the disintegration of feudalism and the advent of its replacement, industrialism. *Industrialisme* meant the triumph of technology over backwardness, of science and reason over superstition and custom. Saint-Simon's vision of the industrial society is almost a carbon copy of John Kenneth Galbraith's (1967) technocracy. E. S. Mason (1931) referred to Saint-Simon's goal as "the rationalisation of industry." What is conveyed by each of these phrases is a coming to the fore in a market economy of the business leader, the economic "expert" whose skills are tempered in the crucible of competition. Saint-Simon's society of producers requires the sort of person who can apply established principles toward the attainment of recognized goals. Ultimately this demands that business is brought into politics and that politicians become producers.

Whether or not a society reorganized along the lines suggested by Saint-Simon or Galbraith would be competitive in the classical sense is problematic. Although Saint-Simon gave the entrepreneur a prominent place in his economic structure, he did not develop the concept beyond what is implied in the notion of a business leader. Nor did he concern himself with economic analysis, per se, which of necessity precedes the task of reorganization. He was content with the economic analysis and the economic policy of Smith and Say. And in the end, his disciples transformed his doctrine into a kind of religion, thus eroding its appeal to serious economists in search of operational tools of analysis.

POSTSCRIPT

Even a cursory review of French economic literature in the eighteenth and early nineteenth centuries reveals that the entrepreneur was regarded as a vital component of a market economy. The development of the concept, however, did not follow strict evolutionist principles. As economists attempted to discover and elucidate the laws of the market, variations in the definition and function of the entrepreneur were introduced, first by one author then by another—even among writers who shared a common language.

On other shores, writers of different languages and cultures also dealt with the concept. We turn our attention next to developments in England and Germany during the high time of classical economics, circa 1776 to 1870.

NOTE

1. One French economist who took exception to Say's theory of entrepreneurship was Courcelle-Seneuil (1813–1892), who insisted that profit is not a wage but is due to the assumption of risk. Knight (1921, p. 25n) attributes to him a glimpse of "the fact that the assumption of a 'risk' of error in one's judgment, inherent in the making of a responsible decision, is a phenomenon of a different character from the assumption of 'risk' in the insurance sense."

5   *DEAD ENDS, DETOURS, AND REDIRECTIONS*

Assuming the burden of the fluctuations in the expenditure which must be made in any business and in the results attained is . . . the distinctive mark of the entrepreneur.

H. von Mangoldt

ENGLISH CUSTOM BEFORE ADAM SMITH

There were three commonly used English equivalents to the French term *entrepreneur* in the eighteenth century: "adventurer," "projector," and "undertaker." The first term was applied in the fifteenth century to merchants operating at some risk, and in the seventeenth century to land speculators, farmers, and those who directed certain public works projects. During the eighteenth century, the term adventurer gradually gave way to the more general term undertaker, which by the time Smith wrote (in 1776), had become synonymous with an ordinary businessman. The term projector was equivalent to the other two in a fundamental sense, but it more often had the pejorative connotation of a cheat and a rogue. The word undertaker was not only used more often but had more varied meanings, and its history more or less paralleled the development of its French counterpart.

At first, *undertaker* simply meant someone who set out to do a job or complete a project, but its meaning eventually channeled into the concept of government contractor—someone who, at his own financial risk, performed a task imposed on him by government. The term was later extended to include those individuals who held exclusive franchises from the Crown or the Parliament, for example, tax farmers, or those individuals commissioned to drain the fens. By and by the government connection was dropped, and the term simply came to designate someone involved in a risky project from which an uncertain profit might be derived (Hoselitz 1960, pp. 240–42). For reasons that are not clear, by the nineteenth century "undertaker" had acquired the special meaning of an arranger of funerals. Partly because of the example provided by Smith, the economic meaning of the term undertaker eventually came to be replaced by the term capitalist.

SMITH, RICARDO, AND THE "UNFORTUNATE LEGACY"

The *locus classicus* of economic analysis in the eighteenth century was Adam Smith's *Inquiry Into the Nature and Causes of the Wealth of Nations* (1776). Although a certified classic in the history of economics, it is notably deficient in one important sense. Smith failed to separate the entrepreneurial decision maker from among the various kinds of "industrious people" in the economy. He made passing references to both projectors and undertakers, but Smith infused neither of these terms with entrepreneurial content.[1] The undertaker was regarded as a mere capitalist, and at that, he was, in Spengler's phrase, "a prudent, cautious, not overly imaginative fellow, who adjusts to circumstances rather than brings about their modification" (1959, pp. 8–9).

Smith observed that the profits of the undertaker constitute a reward for hazarding his stock (capital) in a particular venture. Conforming to customary eighteenth-century usage, Smith linked the projector to speculative enterprises, noting that "establishment of any new manufacture, of any new branch of commerce, or of any new practice in agriculture, is always a speculation, from which the projector promises himself extraordinary profits" (1937, p. 114).

Indirect references to the entrepreneurial role are nevertheless present in Smith's magnum opus. For example, managerial decision making is clearly important in connection with the division of labor. Smith observed:

The owner of the stock which employs a great number of labourers necessarily endeavors, for his own advantage, to make such a proper division and distribution of employment, that they may be enabled to produce the greatest quantity of work possible. (1937, p. 86)

However, Smith refuted Turgot's idea that the labor of organization and direction is a determinant of profit. He declared:

The profits of stock, it may perhaps be thought, are only a different name for the wages of a particular sort of labour, the labour of inspection and direction. They are, however, altogether different, are regulated by quite sufficient principles, and bear no proportion to the quantity, the hardship, or the ingenuity of this supposed labour of inspection and direction. They are regulated altogether by the value of the stock employed, and are greater or smaller in proportion to the extent of this stock. (1937, p. 48)

Smith was correct in his assertion that labor is labor, regardless of who expends it, but while correcting Turgot's mistake, he erred as badly by confounding production goods, capital, profits and interest. Charles Tuttle (1927, pp. 507–8) claims that Smith's failure to differentiate the function of the capitalist from that of the entrepreneur must be attributed to prevailing business practice with which Smith was familiar. In England and France at this time the ownership of capital was prerequisite to becoming the independent head of a business. This fact is reflected in works by Turgot and Smith, each of whom took the ownership of capital for granted; yet Smith gave much stronger emphasis to the ownership of capital as the basis for entrepreneurship.

Smith's refusal to separate the functions of the entrepreneur and capitalist unfortunately set the pattern for the remainder of the classical period. We agree with Fritz Redlich (1966, p. 715), that this was an unfortunate legacy. It implied, among other things, that profit is not legitimate in a capitalist economy. Through David Ricardo, this legacy was bequeathed to Karl Marx, who embellished and continued the idea of the capitalist bogey, that is, the parasitic "extortionist" who sucks profit from the "industrious" people of the economy.

The paradox involved in Smith's treatment (or, more appropriately, nontreatment) of the entrepreneur is further heightened by the fact that he was very sensitive to the effects of innovation in a capitalist society. Indeed, Smith was one of the first economic writers to recognize innovation as a professional activity. In a remark on inventions made by workmen, Smith observed:

Many improvements have been made by the ingenuity of the makers of the machines, when to make them became the business of a peculiar trade; and some by that of those who are called philosophers or men of speculation, whose trade it is not to do anything, but to observe everything; and who, upon that account, are often capable of combining together the powers of the most distant and dissimilar objects. (1937, p. 10)

It is difficult to see how the "philosophers" of this passage are any different from those we call innovative entrepreneurs (for example, a Thomas Edison), yet Smith did not develop this fruitful line of inquiry.

The eighteenth-century inventor (Smith's "philosopher" or "speculator") was an amateur by contemporary standards; yet Smith's view of innovation as professional activity was ahead of its time. He held that innovation is the product of the division of labor, which in turn depends on the extent of the market. Innovation therefore appears first in markets that are enlarged by cheap transportation. Opulence and progress thereafter accompany the division of labor, and with this progress the innovator or inventor becomes more specialized, and "the quantity of science is considerably increased."

Despite this noteworthy advance by the "father of economics," classical economics in general had very little to say about the origin and nature of investment opportunities. This is especially true of Ricardo (1772–1823), who assumed that capitalists act rationally in seeking to maximize profits but who shed no light on the nature of the trouble and risk involved in investing. Although he did not fall into the trap of assuming that all investment was profitable, like most classical economists Ricardo treated innovation as mainly external to the economic system. On occasion he supposed that as wealth increased, eventually all further opportunities for profitable investment would disappear. This stands in marked contrast to the Schumpeterian view, which was the first modern statement of innovation as professional activity within the economic system. Not only the scope but the breadth of entrepreneurial activity and investment opportunity were consequently enlarged in the Schumpeterian system.

There is a sense in which Ricardo is more culpable than Smith for his neglect of the entrepreneur. Smith was acquainted with Quesnay, and he may also have known Turgot's work directly. But aside from a difference in emphasis, Smith did not view the entrepreneur/undertaker in terms much different from his French counterparts. Ricardo, on the other hand, failed entirely to pursue Say's suggestion that the entrepreneur is distinguishable from the other agents of production. Smith could not have done so because his work preceded

Say's, but Say had formalized the term entrepreneur and given it definition some 14 years before Ricardo's *Principles* appeared. Moreover, at least one version of Say's work was available to Ricardo in English during this 14-year period. Yet, as Arthur Cole noted, "not merely is the term [entrepreneur] itself absent in Ricardo's writings, but no concept of business leaders as agents of change (other than as shadowy bearers of technological improvements) is embraced in his treatment of economic princples" (1946, p. 3). It is noteworthy that in the correspondence between Say and Ricardo, neither the nature nor role of the entrepreneur is once mentioned, the usual discussion focusing instead on the topic of value.

JEREMY BENTHAM: THE ENTREPRENEUR AS CONTRACTOR

Ricardo played a major role in setting forth the "research program" that was to occupy the next generation of economists. Consequently, his failure to recognize the entrepreneur as a separate agent of production was a harbinger of later developments in economic theory by classical economists. In the field of public policy, however, one British writer paid considerable attention to the entrepreneur. That writer was Jeremy Bentham (1748–1832), whose ties with France and its intellectual tradition were much stronger than those of his contemporaries.

It is noteworthy that Bentham and Ricardo had different notions about what political economy should be. Ricardo saw political economy as a means to discover general laws of society. For him, economics was a theory detached from practice, whatever might subsequently be its practical consequences. To Ricardo, political economy was a science of laws—laws of equilibrium and laws of progress. By contrast, Bentham understood political economy in much the same way as his contemporary, Smith. He referred to economics as both art and science, and he paid as much attention to the former as he did to the latter. For Bentham, as for Smith, political economy was a branch of politics and legislation, never removed from practice. We cannot be sure whether it was Bentham's large concern for practice as well as theory that induced him to see the importance of the entrepreneur in economic activity. But it is a matter of record that he reproached Smith for his flogging efforts against "projectors."

Like Smith, Bentham understood that the regime most favorable to the development of inventive faculties was one of absolute liberalism. But, unlike Smith, Bentham (1952) defended usurers and projectors as useful sets of men. Both helped to advance the cause of inventive genius, each in his own way. It is something of a puzzle that Smith would, on the one hand, recognize innovation as a professional activity while on the other hand ignore its importance in another context. In his denunciation of usury, Smith failed to see the importance of the innovator. Bentham aptly pointed this out in his *Defence of Usury* (1787), the first publication that brought him public recognition as an economist. There Bentham detailed how laws against usury limit the overall quantity of capital lent and borrowed and how such laws keep away foreign money from domestic capital markets. Both these effects tend to throttle the activities of successful entrepreneurs. Although Bentham used the customary term projector, he was quite precise in his definition of this term as any person who, in the pursuit of wealth, strikes out into any new channel, especially into any channel of invention. He argued that interest rate ceilings tend to discriminate against entrepreneurs of new projects, because, by their novelty, such projects are more risky than those already proven profitable by experience. Moreover, legal restrictions of this sort are powerless to pick out bad projects from good ones.

In pleading the cause of the projectors, Bentham, the inventor of the Panopticon, was to some extent pleading his own case. Panopticon was the name Bentham gave to his idea of a model prison. The concept involved both an architectural and an institutional innovation. Bentham's ideal prison was circular. All the cells were arranged concentrically round a central pavillion, which contained an inspector, or at most a small number of inspectors. From his central position the inspector could see at a glance everything that was going on, yet he was rendered invisible by a system of blinds. In this way, too, outside visitors could inspect the prisoners, as well as the prison's administration, without being seen. According to Bentham, this constant scrutiny of the prisoners would deprive them of the power, and even the will, to do evil. The site that Bentham proposed for his model prison is now occupied by the Tate Gallery in London. Bentham was never able to attract enough backers to make his model prison a reality.

The architectural idea behind the Panopticon was first applied in Russia by Bentham's brother Samuel, who in fact, deserves priority for the idea. Bentham's unique contribution was an administrative innovation that is more to the point of our subject than the general problem of prison reform. Bentham completed the architectural innovation of the Panopticon by introducing an administrative arrangement that involved management by contract. What is especially interesting about this arrangement is the critical way that its success depends on the dynamic activities of the entrepreneur and the proper structuring of economic incentives.

To Bentham, true reform would obtain in prisons only if the administrative plan simultaneously protected convicts against the harshness of their warders and society against the wastefulness of administrators. The choice, as he saw it, was between contract management and trust management. The differences are as follows:

Contract-management is management by a man who treats with the government, and takes charge of the convicts at so much a head and applies their time and industry to his personal profit, as does a master with his apprentices. Trust-management is management by a single individual or by a committee, who keep up the establishment at the public expense, and pay into the treasury the products of the convicts' work. (Halévy 1955, p. 84)

In Bentham's mind, the latter arrangement did not provide the proper junction of interest and duty on the part of the entrepreneur. Its success therefore depends on "public interest" as a motivating factor. Bentham, like his proclaimed mentor, Smith, had much more confidence in individual self-interest as the spur to human action. The beauty of contract management was that it brought about an *artificial* identity of interests between the public on the one hand and the entrepreneur on the other. The entrepreneur in this case was an independent contractor who "purchased," through competitive bid, the right to run the prison, thereby also acquiring title to whatever profits might be earned by the application of convict labor. Such an entrepreneur-manager could maximize his long-term gains by preserving the health and productivity of his worker-convicts. In this manner public interest became entwined with private interest.

In 1787, Bentham completed the idea of contract management by a new administrative arrangement: He thought that life insurance offered an excellent means of joining the interest of one man to the preservation of a number of men. He therefore proposed that after consulting the appropriate mortality tables, the entrepreneur (prison manager) should be given a fixed sum of money for each convict due to die that year in prison, on condition that at the end of the year he must pay back the same sum for each convict who had actually died in prison. The difference would be profit for the entrepreneur, who would thereby have an economic incentive to lower the average mortality rate in his prison (Bentham 1962, vol. IV, p. 53).

Aside from the fact that Bentham was virtually alone among British classical economists in his repeated emphasis on the entrepreneur as an agent of economic progress, it is noteworthy that his administrative arrangement of contract management recast the entrepreneur in the position of government contractor, that is, a franchisee who undertakes financial risk in order to obtain an uncertain profit. Bentham also explicitly tied his notion of entrepreneur-contractor to the act of invention. He defended contract management as the proper form of prison administration on the ground that it is a progressive innovation and should therefore be rewarded accordingly, no less than an inventor is rewarded for his invention (1962, vol. IV, p. 47).

JOHN STUART MILL AND THE DECLINE
OF BRITISH CLASSICAL ECONOMICS

The work of John Stuart Mill (1806–1873) is a watershed in British classical economics. It consists of a mature statement of the economic paradigm first enunciated by Smith and successively refined and developed by Ricardo, Thomas Malthus, Nassau Senior, and others. It is also a kind of bridge between the economics of the old school (1776–1870) and the new (1871–1920).

Mill contributed little that was new to the theory of entrepreneurship. He lamented the fact that "undertaker" did not adequately convey the desired economic meaning, and he noted the superiority of the French term for this purpose (1965, p. 406n). But throughout his *Principles*, Mill spoke somewhat ambiguously of the entrepreneur and of his economic reward. According to Mill, the function of the entrepreneur is variously, direction, control, and superintendence. In one place he observed that the qualities of direction and superintendence are always in short supply (1965, p. 108), and in another, he suggested that superior business talents such as these always receive a kind of rent alongside ordinary profits (1965, p. 476), thus approaching H. K. von Mangoldt's important innovation on the theory (see below). In the final analysis, he offered no clear-cut distinction between the capitalist and the entrepreneur, insisting that the return to the latter is composed of a risk premium and a wage of superintendence. This view was representative of most treatments by British classical economists.

If pressed, individual writers of the period would probably have denied it, but the impression left by British classical economics is that each business practically runs by itself. Undertakers are rather passive capitalists who accumulate capital, hire workers, and supervise production, with a view to making a profit. There is no sense of a dynamic economic agent either inventing or seizing profit opportunities that arise from new knowledge, new combinations of productive factors, new products, new marketing techniques, and so forth.

Schumpeter (1954, p. 555) claims that Say was the first to assign the entrepreneur a distinct position in the economic process apart from the capitalist, but even Say did not make full use of his own insight, nor did he see clearly all of its analytic possibilities. On Mill's home turf, Bentham was the first Englishman to offer innovative insights beyond Say, but he was more concerned with institutional reform than with the development of a core of analytic principles that were strictly economic. Mill had read Bentham and Say, but he did not follow the suggestions on entrepreneurship advanced by either writer. He kept the entrepreneur in the background of his distribution theory by focusing mainly on land, labor, and capital as agents of production. By implication, this suggests that the entrepreneur is either a special laborer, or a combination of laborer and capitalist. Mill did not seriously entertain the idea of the entrepreneur as innovator. Where he discussed the labor of invention and discovery, for example, Mill treated its reward as merely a kind of wage.

Mill outlined the capitalist's return as the sum of an opportunity cost for postponing consumption (i.e., Senior's "abstinence"), plus an indemnity for risk of capital, plus the "wages of superintendence." He asserted further that the wages of superintendence are not regulated by the same principle as wages in general. Specifically, he maintained that the wages of superintendence are not advanced out of capital, like the wages of other workers, but arise in profit, which is not realized until production is completed.

In Mill's time, the wages of labor were explained by the wages-fund doctrine, which viewed the source of wages as capital (i.e., accumulation) that is advanced to workers prior to realization of final output. In this view, the total amount that can be paid to labor is limited by the amount of capital previously accumulated. Mill's distinction between ordinary wages and the wages of superintendence therefore implies that there is no such limit on the wages of superintendence. But we are still left with the somewhat unhappy alliance (identity?) of the entrepreneur and the capitalist. Because of this functional "merger" British classical economics offered no focal point for viewing the pivotal role of the entrepreneur in the economic process.

GERMAN PERFORMANCES IN
THE CLASSICAL PERIOD

Circumstances were different in Germany, where the classical period began around 1800, with the substitution of political economy for German cameral science. The early writers in this tradition were Ludwig von Jakob and Julius Graf von Soden. By 1814, Say's *Treatise* had been translated and was beginning to make an impact on German economics.

The attempt to establish the entrepreneur's profit as a distinctive functional share in the theory of income distribution accelerated faster in Germany than in either France or England. Major advances were made by J. H. von Thünen (1785–1850) and H. K. von Mangoldt (1824–1858), with earlier help from Gottlieb Hufeland (1760–1817), Friedrich Hermann (1795–1868), and especially Adolph Riedel (1809–1872).

Hufeland (1807) recognized that every wage contains a premium for scarcity. He generalized this idea to explain entrepreneurial profit as a special kind of wage consisting of the rent-of-ability. Hermann's (1832) theoretical economics undermined the wages-fund theory by asserting that all factor returns are ultimately paid from consumers' income. Like Hufeland he generalized the concept of rent to all factors, including the entrepreneur. Like Say, he viewed the entrepreneur as one who organizes production within the institutional structure of a firm.

Riedel (1838) extended Cantillon's conception of the entrepreneur as the economic agent who himself bears uncertainty in order that uncertainty be reduced for others (through the establishment of fixed-price contracts). He perceived that uncertainty is inevitable in the acquisition of income and that the entrepreneur provides a service to income earners who are risk-averse and who would therefore willingly trade uncertainty for the security of a "sure thing." As a supplier of "certainty," the entrepreneur is rewarded for his foresight or penalized for lack of it. If he sells goods at a price above his contracted fixed-input costs, he gains; if not, he loses. Riedel also explored the notion of the entrepreneur as innovator, and as organizer of "team production." By connecting the problems of the organization of firms with the entrepreneurial function of reducing income uncertainty for certain inputs, he anticipated (as did Mangoldt) the nature of transactions costs later expounded by Ronald Coase (see Chapter 10).

Thünen is best known in the history of economics for his contributions to location theory, but in the second volume of *The Isolated State* (1850) he set forth an explanation of profit that clearly distinguished the return of the entrepreneur from that of the capitalist. What Thünen labeled "entrepreneurial gain" is profit minus (1) interest on invested capital, (2) insurance against business losses, and (3) the wages of management. This residual represents, for Thünen, a return to entrepreneurial risk. This last item Thünen identified as uninsurable risk, insofar as "there exists no insurance company that will cover all and every risk connected with a business. A part of the risk must always be accepted by the entrepreneur" (1960, p. 246).

As Kanbur (1980) has argued, opportunity costs provide the basis for measuring this element of risk. Thünen seems to have had the same argument in mind when he wrote:

He who has enough means to pay to get some knowledge and education for public service has a choice to become either a civil servant or, if equally suited for both kinds of jobs, to become an industrial entrepreneur. If he takes the first job, he is guaranteed subsistence for life; if he chooses the latter, an unfortunate economic situation may take all his property, and then his fate becomes that of a worker for daily wages. Under such unequal expectations for the future what could motivate him to become an entrepreneur if the probability of gain were not much greater than that of loss? (1960, p. 247)

Thünen clearly appreciated the difference between management and entrepreneurship. He maintained that the effort of an entrepreneur working on his own account was different from that of a paid substitute ("manager"), even if they have the same knowledge and ability. The entrepreneur is open to the anxiety and agitation that accompanies his business gamble; he spends many sleepless nights preoccupied with the single thought of how to avoid catastrophe, whereas the paid substitute, if he has worked well during the day and finds himself tired in the evening, can sleep soundly, secure in the knowledge of having performed his duty. Anyone who has nursed along a new enterprise knows precisely of what Thünen speaks.

What is especially interesting about Thünen's treatment is how he turns the discussion from the trials of the entrepreneur into a kind of "crucible" theory of the development of entrepreneurial talent. The sleepless nights of the entrepreneur are not unproductive; it is then that the entrepreneur makes his plans and arrives at solutions for avoiding business failure. Adversity in the business world thereby becomes a training ground for the entrepreneur. As Thünen put it:

Necessity is the mother of invention; and so the entrepreneur through his troubles will become an inventor and explorer in his field. So, as the invention of a new and useful machine rightly gets the surplus which its application provides in comparison with an older machine, and this surplus is the compensation for his invention, in the same way what the entrepreneur brings about by greater mental effort in comparison with the paid manager is compensation for his industry, diligence, and ingenuity. (1960, p. 248)

What makes this a significant step forward in the theory of entrepreneurship is the fact that Thünen successfully married the separate strands of entrepreneurial theory that, on the one hand, characterized the entrepreneur as risk bearer (Cantillon, Mill), and, on the other hand, portrayed him as innovator (Baudeau, Bentham). Economic analysis having come this far by 1850, we may well question whether Schumpeter took a step backward in the next century by excluding risk bearing from the nature of entrepreneurship, confining its meaning instead solely to innovative activity (see Chapter 8).

Thünen was quite explicit about the fact that there are two elements in entrepreneurial income: a return to "entrepreneurial risk" and a return to ingenuity. Labeling the sum of these two as "business profit," Thünen drew a succinct and precise distinction between entrepreneurship and capital use:

Capital will give results, and is in the strict sense of the term capital, only if used productively; on the degree of this usefulness depends the rate of interest at which we lend capital. Productive use presupposes an industrial enterprise and an entrepreneur. The enterprise gives the entrepreneur a net yield after compensating for all expenses and costs. This net yield has two parts, business profits and capital use. (1960, p. 249)

A second landmark performance on the subject of the entrepreneur was produced by Mangoldt, professor at the universities of Göttingen and Freiburg. Mangoldt's writings remain inaccessible to those unfamiliar with the German language, but we know of his contributions indirectly through Knight (1921), Schumpeter (1954), Hutchison (1953), and Hennings (1980). Knight attributed to Mangoldt "a most careful and exhaustive analysis of profit" (1921, p. 27), and Schumpeter judged his work on entrepreneurship "the most important advance since Say" (1954, p. 556n).

Mangoldt attempted to reform Hermann's theory, which sought the essential characteristic of entrepreneurship in the personal activity of entrepreneurs. Hermann maintained that certain kinds of labor are inseparable from the nature of entrepreneurship and if these tasks are delegated to anyone else, the delegator ceases to be an entrepreneur. Among these tasks Hermann listed the assembling of capital, the supervision of business, the securing of credit and trade connections, and the assumption of risk connected with the prospect of irregular gains.

Mangoldt discarded Hermann's first three entrepreneurial tasks as inessential to a "pure" notion of entrepreneurship. Although entrepreneurs customarily participate in their own enterprises with their own capital and personal supervision, Mangoldt argued that these services could be furnished just as well by salaried labor. What remains from Hermann's list is risk bearing. According to Mangoldt, "That which alone is inseparable from the concept of the entrepreneur is, on the one hand, owning the output of the undertaking–control over the product brought forth, and, on the other hand, assuming responsibility for whatever losses may occur" (1907, p. 41).

Mangoldt's theory of entrepreneurship was production-oriented and risk-centered. He distinguished between "production to order" and "production for the market." The former is safe because service and payment are simultaneous, thereby eliminating the uncertainty of changing market conditions between the start of production and sale of the final product. The latter is speculative because the product is destined for exchange on a market of uncertain demand and unknown price. Mangoldt found this distinction useful, even though it is imprecise:

Strictly interpreted, every possibility of a change in the subjective estimate of the service, or the remuneration, offers such an uncertainty; and, on that account, since such a possibility is excluded only by a perfect simultaneity of service and payment, every business which needs for its carrying through any time whatever, could not, in the strictest sense of the word, be undertaken to order. (1907, p. 37)

The significance of the distinction is that it provides a means of discussing degrees of risk that may befall the entrepreneur. By Mangoldt's reckoning, those enterprises that require the longest time to bring their products to the point of final sale involve the most uncertainty, whereas those that involve the shortest time require the least amount of entrepreneurship. Risk and uncertainty go to the heart of the matter. The distinctive mark of Mangoldt's entrepreneur is that he assumes the burden of the fluctuations in expenditure that must be made in any business and in the consequent outcome of the enterprise. In this respect Mangoldt stood squarely in the tradition inaugurated by Cantillon.

Mangoldt also developed the notion that entrepreneurial profit is the rent of ability, and he insisted that the entrepreneur be treated as a separate factor of production. He divided entrepreneurial income into three parts: a premium on uninsurable risks; entrepreneur interest and wages, including only payments for special forms of capital or productive effort that did not admit of exploitation by anyone other than the owner; and entrepreneur rents, that is, payments for differential abilities or assets not held by anyone else. Alfred Marshall (1961, vol. II, p. 462) took special note of this last item, citing Mangoldt approvingly in his development of the principle of quasi-rent.

Mangoldt's theory did not concentrate on an ideal type of entrepreneur but rather on the decisions he must make in an uncertain, competitive environment: the choice of techniques, the allocation of productive factors, and the marketing of production. Although he recognized that successful innovation is part of entrepreneurship, Mangoldt nevertheless expressed more interest in the allocative function of the entrepreneur. His contribution therefore belongs more to the static theory of resource allocation than to the dynamic theory of growth and development.

Both Thünen and Mangoldt were important anticipators of Knight (see Chapter 7), who in the next century revived Cantillon's idea of the entrepreneur as risk bearer. Thünen's contribution may be judged the more significant of the two, however, insofar as it combined elements of risk bearing and innovation in a way that pointed past the concept of entrepreneurship that has until recently dominated twentieth-century literature on the subject. On the other hand, as Tuttle asserts, after Mangoldt's treatment, "economists could no longer consider the function [of the entrepreneur] as a mere incident to some other function, or ignore it altogether, as had been the case hitherto" (1927, p. 518).

NOTE

1. According to Reekie (1984), elements of entrepreneurial activity *are* present in Smith; just not recognized by Smith. The propensity to truck, barter, and exchange is itself an entrepreneurial activity, that is, an activity involving coordination of resources and perception of opportunity.

6   *THE ENTREPRENEUR RESURRECTED*

The entrepreneur is any legal owner of an enterprise.

Friedrich von Wieser

THE NEOCLASSICAL ERA

In its infancy, neoclassical economics turned away from the macroeconomic concerns of growth and income distribution as primary issues, and directed its attention toward the fundamental laws of price formation. This redirection was ushered in by a radical new emphasis on the role of individual demand. Neoclassical economics placed greater emphasis on the marginal utility evaluations of individuals than on cost considerations in the calculation of economic value. With one or two notable exceptions, economic analysis after 1870 became increasingly abstract and mechanistic. The economic problem came to be perceived as the allocation of certain scarce means among given ends, rather than the selection of the ends themselves. In this era, no longer did the great macroeconomic issues of the classical period (e.g., population, capital supply, economic growth) dominate economic inquiry.

The new economic analysis was developed by a novel breed of professional economists who, unlike their predecessors of the earlier period, received university training and took up teaching positions in the new discipline. Consequently they were less firmly rooted in the parent discipline of philosophy and simultaneously more open to the applications of mathematics to economic reasoning. All of this underlay the subtle change of terminology by which "economics" undermined and eventually replaced the older phrase "political economy."

Although the issues of the new economics were fundamentally the same, three distinct viewpoints vied for supremacy during the neoclassical era. These three approaches may be loosely identified as Austrian, French, and British. Each had a different intellectual tradition behind it, and each emphasized different things in its redirection of economic analysis. Of the three, the Austrian approach proved most fertile for advancing the theory of the entrepreneur.

THE AUSTRIAN SCHOOL

With the publication of his *Principles of Economics* in 1871, Carl Menger (1840–1921) established himself as the founder and early leader of a distinctively Austrian school that later included two able disciples, Friedrich von Wieser (1851–1926) and Eugen von Böhm-Bawerk (1851–1914). The central concern of Menger's economics was to establish the subjectivist perspective of human valuation as the starting point of economic theory. In the subjectivist view, economic change arises from an individual's awareness and understanding of circumstances rather than from the circumstances, per se. Thus Menger's analysis, as both Erich Streissler (1972) and Israel Kirzner (1979a) have pointed out, relied heavily on the role of knowledge in individual decisions.

Although Menger's theory of production is subservient to his theory of value, it is to the theory of production that one must look for an appreciation of the entrepreneurial role.

Menger's theory of production starts with the general theory of the good. For something to be a good in the economic sense requires recognition of the causal connection between useful things and the satisfaction of human needs, as well as action taken to direct the useful things to this satisfaction. In other words, the goods character of any useful thing is not innate; it must be acquired through human action, that is, recognition of a need, capability of satisfying that need, and action taken to do so. In the Austrian framework, goods can be ranked according to their causal connections. To use Menger's (1950, p. 56) example, the bread we eat, the flour from which it is baked, the grain milled into flour, and the field on which the grain is grown are all goods. But some goods serve individual needs directly, and some stand in a more remote causal connection. The former are called goods of "lower order"; the latter, goods of "higher order." The farther removed a good is from satisfying a want directly, the higher the number assigned to it in Menger's scale of goods-ordering. Thus bread is a good of first order because it satisfies hunger directly. Flour is a second-order good because it is one step removed from the direct satisfaction of need. The grain from which flour is milled, along with the mill and labor expended on it, are third-order goods. The field, farmers, and equipment used to grow grain are fourth-order goods, and so on.

From the foregoing we can see that to designate the order of a particular good is to indicate that in some particular employment it has a closer or more distant causal relationship with the satisfaction of a human need. For Menger, the ultimate goods character of higher order goods depends on the power to transform goods of higher order into goods of lower order. Economic production is the process by which this transformation takes place and by which the goods of lower order are directed finally into the satisfaction of human needs. This process is inseparable from the idea of time. Over time improvements in technology and transportation tend

continually to shorten the time between phases of transform-
ing higher order goods into lower order goods, but the time
gaps never disappear completely. It is impossible to transform
higher order goods into lower order goods by a mere wave of
the hand. Production is never instantaneous.

Menger's conception of the entrepreneur, although never
elaborated in any great detail, fits into the vision of production just outlined. This general theory of production leads to
a conceptualization of the entrepreneur as one who must deal
with the intertemporal coordination of the factors of production (that is, higher order goods). Menger recognized that
industry is vertically disintegrated and that somebody has to
align productive resources over time. That somebody is the
entrepreneur. Ironically, the entrepreneur's own technical
labor services are usually among the higher order goods he
has at his command for purposes of production. Nevertheless,
it is not the supply of such services that makes one an entrepreneur; it is instead his calculating and decision-making abilities that make his function unique. According to Menger,

Entrepreneurial activity includes: (a) obtaining *information* about the
economic situation; (b) economic *calculation*—all the various computations that must be made if a production process is to be efficient; (c)
the *act of will* by which goods of higher order are assigned to a particular production process; and finally (d) *supervision* of the execution of
the production plan so that it may be carried through as economically
as possible. (1950, p. 160)

An obvious corollary of Menger's conception of entrepreneurial activity is that the entrepreneur must face uncertainty
with regard to the quantity and quality of final goods he can
produce with the goods of higher order in his possession. The
degree of uncertainty faced by the entrepreneur depends on
the extent of his knowledge of the productive process and
upon the degree of control he exercises over it. Menger recognized this fact and underscored its importance:

Human uncertainty about the quantity and quality of the product of the whole causal process is greater the larger the number of elements involved in any way in the production of consumption goods which we either do not understand or over which, even understanding them, we have no control. . . . This uncertainty . . . is of the greatest practical significance in human economy. (1950, p. 71)

Menger did not attempt to link the entrepreneur with the capitalist, and, indeed, it would have been a step backward for entrepreneurial theory had he done so. But his position with regard to risk bearing is curious, especially in the face of repeated emphasis on the significance of uncertainty in economic affairs. Despite the fact that the entrepreneur must continually contend with uncertainty in the process of production, Menger held that risk bearing cannot be the essential function of the entrepreneur. Noting his departure from Mangoldt on this issue, Menger (1950, p. 161) asserted that risk is insignificant to entrepreneurship because in the final analysis the chance of loss is offset by the chance of gain.[1]

It is interesting to speculate whether Menger's treatment of risk vis-à-vis entrepreneurship influenced a later "Austrian," Joseph Schumpeter (see Chapter 8), who also denied risk bearing as an essential characteristic of entrepreneurship. The outcome of such speculation remains problematic, but Schumpeter's vision went beyond Menger's in the sense that his entrepreneur was a driving force in the process of economic development. In fact, Schumpeter virtually stood Menger on his head. Whereas Menger (1950) saw economic progress as leading to the development of entrepreneurial activity, Schumpeter viewed entrepreneurial activity as leading to economic progress.

Wieser was a student of Karl Knies's but a follower of Menger's. He extended Menger's ideas and added several important dimensions to his entrepreneur, among them leadership, alertness, and risk bearing. Wieser defined the entrepreneur in a "legalistic" but otherwise sweeping fashion:

[T]he entrepreneur . . . is the director by legal right and at the same time by virtue of his active participation in the economic management of his enterprise. He is a leader in his own right. He is the legal representative of the operation, the owner of the material productive goods, creditor for all accounts receivable and debtor for all accounts payable. As a lessor or lessee he is obligated or privileged. He is the employer under all contracts for work and labor. . . . His economic leadership commences with the establishment of the enterprise; he supplies not only the necessary capital but originates the idea, elaborates and puts into operation the plan, and engages collaborators. When the enterprise is established, he becomes its manager technically as well as commercially. (1927, p. 324)

As is apparent from this passage, Wieser tried to bring everything connected with the theory and practice of enterprise under his umbrellalike definition of the entrepreneur. He spoke of entrepreneurs as the "great personalities" of capitalism: "bold technical innovators, organizers with a keen knowledge of human nature, farsighted bankers, reckless speculators, the world-conquering directors of the trusts" (1927, p. 327).

This is painting with a broad brush. Not only is Wieser's multifarious entrepreneur a director, leader, employer, owner, capitalist, and innovator, "he must [also] possess the quick perception that seizes new terms in current transactions as his affairs develop; [and] he must possess the independent forcefulness to regulate his business according to his views." Finally, he must have the courage to accept risk and be driven forward by "the joyful power to create" (1927, p. 324).

Wieser's discussion touched themes that would be expounded again in the next two generations of entrepreneurial theories. Schumpeter (see Chapter 8) zeroed in on the innovating spirit and the creativity of entrepreneurs. Kirzner (see Chapter 9) elaborated the perceptiveness theme. As a rule, modern theories of entrepreneurship have averted the multifarious personality of the entrepreneur in favor of a more narrowly defined figure. Wieser, too, eventually admitted that institutional changes, primarily in forms of business organization, had gradually transformed the notion of entrepreneur to a mere legal concept. In the wake of such changes Wieser declared: "The requirement of economic management is no longer fulfilled in all cases. Today the enterprise is a voluntary community of commercial operation in the money economy subject to one entrepreneur. It may be a unified group of such operations. The entrepreneur is any legal owner of an enterprise" (1927, p. 328).

The third member of the Austrian triumvirate, Böhm-Bawerk wrote very little about the entrepreneur, concerning himself primarily with the theory of capital and interest. Schumpeter (1954, p. 893) has alluded to Böhm-Bawerk's uncertainty theory of profits, in which the source of entrepreneurs' profits is that things do not work out as planned. According to the theory, persistence of positive profits in a firm is a consequence of superior judgement in the face of uncertainty. We also have it on Murray Rothbard's (1985) authority that Böhm-Bawerk clearly identified the entrepreneur with the capitalist and that he in no way suggested that they could be separated. Be that as it may, Böhm-Bawerk did not develop his theory of profit and loss to any great extent, leaving this task to be accomplished by his student Mises (see Chapter 9) and by the U.S. economist Knight.

LÉON WALRAS

One of the most panoramic and unique visions of economic theory was exercised by the French economist Léon Walras (1834–1910), who elaborated the all-pervasive interdependence of economic affairs. The theory of general, static equilibrium that he developed shows us a state of ultimate and timeless adjustment maintained by the competitive self-interest of the individual suppliers of productive services. In this world each productive service contributes technically and essentially to the production, transport, and sale of goods, thereby earning each day that amount by which the withdrawal of one such productive unit would reduce the daily output of the system as a whole. Furthermore, in this analytic system the total of all the payments to the suppliers of productive services exactly exhausts their total product.

Walras' lasting contribution to economic theory was architectonic, that is, it was more a contribution of form than of substance. He constructed an elegant system of mathematical equations to represent the totality of the economic system and to emphasize the interdependence of its constituent parts. The actual numbers (i.e., coefficients) that enter these equations in specific circumstances were left to others to discover.

Ostensibly, Walras considered the entrepreneur an important figure. In his *Elements of Pure Economics*, he carefully delineated four classes of productive factors, thus setting the mode of modern practice. His disquisition is reminiscent of Cantillon's three-class presentation of landowners, workers, and entrepreneurs, with the important difference that Walras recognized the capitalist apart from either the landowner or the entrepreneur:

Let us call the holder of land, whoever he may be, a *landowner*, the holder of personal faculties a *worker* and the holder of capital proper a *capitalist*. In addition, let us designate by the term *entrepreneur* a fourth person, entirely distinct from those just mentioned, whose role it is to lease land from the landowner, hire personal faculties from the labo·er, and borrow capital from the capitalist, in order to combine the three productive services in agriculture, industry or trade. It is undoubtedly true that, in real life, the same person may assume two, three, or even all four of the above-defined roles. In fact, the different ways in which these roles may be combined give rise to different types of enterprise. However that may be, the roles themselves, even when performed by the same individual, still remain distinct. From the scientific point of view, we must keep these roles separate and avoid both the error of the English economists who identify the entrepreneur with the capitalist and the error of a certain number of French economists who look upon the entrepreneur as a worker charged with the special task of managing a firm. (1954, p. 222)

As the above passage indicates, Walras' argument with the English economists concerned a point of scientific method more than a matter of substance. His point was that although in practice the functions of capitalist and entrepreneur may frequently be merged, in theory they must be treated separately in order to advance clear thinking about the nature and consequences of each.

Surprisingly, Walras' criticism of his countrymen was more severe. He accused Say of misunderstanding the very nature of the entrepreneurial function, declaring that "this person [the entrepreneur] is absent from his [Say's] theory" (1954, pp. 425–26). In view of Say's generally recognized preeminence in the history of entrepreneurial theory, this is an astounding indictment. Yet Walras defended his position by excluding the activities of coordination and supervision from the entrepreneur's functions. Those activities, he argued repeatedly, are part of routine management and are therefore rewarded by the payment of the wages of management (Walker 1986, p. 5).[2]

A study of Walras' correspondence shows that he maintained his position on the entrepreneur consistently over a long period of time. In his *Eléments*, first published in 1874, he characterized the entrepreneur as an intermediary between production and consumption, an equilibrating agent who is spurred on by profit opportunities in the marketplace. Profit opportunities exist whenever selling price is greater than costs of production. Thus it would appear that the province of the entrepreneur is disequilibrium. In the manner of Cantillon, Walras described the role of the entrepreneur in adjusting supplies in line with manifest demands:

[I]f the selling price of a product exceeds the cost of the productive services for certain firms and a *profit* results, entrepreneurs will flow towards this branch of production or expand their output, so that the quantity of the product [on the market] will increase, its price fall, and the difference between price and cost will be reduced; and, if [on the contrary], the cost of the productive services exceeds the selling price for certain firms, so that a *loss* results, entrepreneurs will leave this branch of production or curtail their output, so that the quantity of the product [on the market] will decrease, its price will rise and the difference between price and cost will again be reduced. (1954, p. 225)

In 1887 Walras wrote to Francis Walker that "the definition of the entrepreneur is, in my opinion, the thing that binds all of economics together" and he proceeded to elaborate his conception of this important resource:

I consider [the entrepreneur] exclusively as the person who buys productive services on the market for services and sells products on the market for products, thus obtaining either a profit or a loss. If he owns some of the land or the capital goods that are used in his firm or if he takes part in the capacity of a director or otherwise in the operation of the transformation of services into products, he is then by virtue of that activity in actuality a landowner, capitalist, or worker, and combines their distinct functions with his own. As a matter of actual practice, for the entrepreneur to combine them is frequent and perhaps even generally necessary; but his doing so ought, I believe, to be put to one side for the purposes of theoretical investigation. (1965, Vol. II, p. 212)

Walras repeated his position on the entrepreneur several year later, in a letter to his disciple, Vilfredo Pareto, explaining how he differed from Marshall on the subject. "Marshall reasons mainly by assumption that the owner of services is a worker who takes it upon himself to make goods and sell them," wrote Walras, whereas "I interpose the entrepreneur as a distinct person whose role is essentially that of demanding services and selling products" (1965, Vol. II, p. 629).

We may take this evidence as confirmation of the fact that the entrepreneur held a prominent place in Walras' view of the world as it actually operates. The extent to which Walras integrated the function of the entrepreneur into the core of his analytical system is another matter. At issue is the idealized nature of Walras' theoretic model and whether it bears any resemblance to the practice of the real world. William Jaffé, a leading Walrasian scholar, and to a lesser extent, Schumpeter, a great admirer of Walras, occupy one extreme in this debate. At the other extreme are Michio Morishima and Donald Walker, the latter a former student of Jaffé.

Walras himself clouded the picture by introducing the "zero-profit entrepreneur" into his model, which is a model of static, general equilibrium without elements of time or uncertainty. Since the entrepreneur neither gains nor loses in competitive equilibrium, his raison d'être disappears in that state. In order to arrive at a determinate mathematical solution, Walras expunged all of the things from his model that give force and range to entrepreneurial action. The result was a theoretic construct that worked like a predictable, impersonal, and frictionless machine. In G. L. S. Shackle's phrase, it was an "inhuman model" (1955, p. 91), incapable of conveying the full range of economic activity. On this account, Schumpeter (1954, p. 893) concluded that Walras's contribution to the theory of entrepreneurship was essentially negative.

Morishima (1977) attempted to establish the centrality of the entrepremeur in Walras' theoretic model, but he was roundly criticized by Jaffé, who asserted, correctly we believe, that "in his whole theoretical construct, Walras deliberately abstracted from uncertainty." This explains the absence of the entrepreneur, *qua* entrepreneur, from the Walrasian model in its 'normal' operation (1980, p. 535). Jaffé concluded that "as for the role of the entrepreneur in Walras' analytical model, the *Eléments* restricted it to that of arbitrageur, and nothing else" (1980, pp. 529–30). Jaffé's position has been challenged by Walker (1986, p. 18), who asserts that Walras made important and lasting contributions to the theory of the entrepreneur, and that Schumpeter (see Chapter 8) built his own novel concept of the entrepreneur on a Walrasian foundation.

It seems clear on this recent evidence that Walras had an unambiguous notion of real world entrepreneurs, and that he assigned them great importance in the practical world of business. But we agree with Jaffé that Walras' theoretic model systematically eliminated, by assumption (and perhaps by necessity), the centrality of the entrepreneur.[3] As theory goes, Walras' general equilibrium system was a momentous contribution. But it does not provide a congenial environment for the entrepreneur, Walras' otherwise promising remarks about him notwithstanding.

ALFRED MARSHALL AND HIS CIRCLE

We have seen how the English variant of classical economics (Smith-Ricardo-Mill) tended to conflate the roles of capitalist and entrepreneur. For its part, British neoclassical value theory did not develop a theory of enterprise, and only grudgingly did it yield a theory of capital. Consequently, the introduction of marginal utility theory did not limit the range of possible differences of opinion concerning the entrepreneur. The new economics took ends as given, explained allocation of scarce resources to meet these given ends, and focused attention on equilibrium results rather than on adjustment processes. It therefore left no room for entrepreneurial action. The entrepreneur became a mere automaton, a passive onlooker with no real scope for individual decision making. Certain British writers kept alive the concept, however, so that the entrepreneur remained, at least sub rosa, in economic theory.

The leading British economist at the turn of the century was Alfred Marshall (1842-1924), who pioneered a synthesis between the economics of the classical and neoclassical periods. Over a span of 30 years, from 1890 to 1920, Marshall dominated British theoretical economics and its pedagogy. His approach to the meaning and function of the "undertaker" and the "business leader" was influenced by the principles of biological evolution expounded by Charles Darwin and Alfred Wallace. This colored his conception of the entrepreneur, whose peculiar skill and ability, he argued, are shaped by an economic struggle for survival in the competitive marketplace.

Marshall elaborated a concept of entrepreneurship that is rooted in the writings of Say and Mill, but is more expansive than either's theory. The core of his concept remained steadfast, but at the periphery its meaning evolved over time. Marshall (1920b, pp. 356, 358) described the elements of "business genius" as alertness, sense of proportion, strength of reasoning, coordination, innovation, and willingness to take risks. He argued that this combination of abilities could be acquired through experience, but not taught by formal education.

In his writings, Marshall reserved a special place for the human agent that *directs* rather than follows economic circumstances. He divided entrepreneurs into two classes, active and passive. Active entrepreneurs are "those who open out new and improved methods of business," whereas passive entrepreneurs are "those who follow beaten tracks" (1920a, p. 597). He made it clear that entrepreneurs of the latter group receive "wages of superintendence," but he carefully elaborated the elements of superintendence so as to add greater substance to Mill's notion of entrepreneurship. However, he reserved his main attention for the active entrepreneur, whose reward is subject to risk. The venturesome entrepreneur cannot avoid risk, because he directs capital and labor to an uncertain end. In order to be successful, therefore, he must be capable of conceiving "wise and far reaching policies, and . . . carry[ing] them out calmly and resolutely" (Marshall 1920a, p. 606).

At bottom, Marshall's entrepreneur was a business manager, although he used the term management to mean more than mere superintendence. Following Charles Darwin, Marshall argued that professional business managers emerge as a special

group from an evolutionary process which is driven by specialization and division of labor. This "Darwinism" may explain
Marshall's inability or unwillingness to tie the entrepreneur to
a single function or set of abilities. The concept itself seems
to evolve endlessly in Marshall's writings and in the final analysis, he placed more emphasis on the existence and necessity
of business ability than on its essence.

In his early work, Marshall stressed duty as an important
stimulus to human action. But his faith in the widespread
application of this Victorian virtue dwindled during the
1880s. After 1890, Marshall placed the chief responsibility
for the economic and moral progress of society on the rest-
less, farsighted, pioneering, but unsung entrepreneur. By
1907, duty had receded farther into the background, and
Marshall was extolling the entrepreneur for his *imagination* as
well as his leadership:

Men of this class live in constantly shifting visions, fashioned in their
own brains, of various routes to their desired end; of the difficulties
which nature will oppose to them on each route, and of the contrivances
by which they hope to get the better of her opposition. This imagination gains little credit with the people, because it is not allowed to run
riot; its strength is disciplined by a stronger will; and its highest glory is
to have attained great ends by means so simple that no one will know,
and none but experts will even guess, how a dozen other expedients,
each suggesting as much brilliancy to the hasty observer, were set aside
in favour of it. (1925, pp. 332-33)

In a purely analytical sense, the most important contribution Marshall made to the theory of entrepreneurship was to
extend Mangoldt's notion of rent-of-ability, though he did
not, as Schumpeter (1954, p. 894) points out, restrict the
idea to the entrepreneur. Freeing himself from the analytical
impediments of the classical wages–fund doctrine, Marshall
attempted to cut through the amorphous nature of "labour"
to capture the uniqueness of individual ability. Observation
and experience told him that "business genius" was unevenly

distributed, and that unique skills received a kind of surplus, or rent:

[T]he class of business undertakers contains a disproportionately large number of persons with high natural ability; since, in addition to the able men born within its ranks it includes also a large share of the best natural abilities born in the lower ranks of industry. And thus while profits on capital invested in education is a specially important element in the incomes of professional men taken as a class, the rent of rare natural abilities may be regarded as a specially important element in the income of business men, so long as we consider them as individuals. (1920a, p. 623)

Marshall's tendency to speak of entrepreneurs sometimes as a class and sometimes as individuals has not helped the cause of clear thinking on the subject. For example, Frederick Harbison asserts that Marshall's notion of the entrepreneur applies not to a single individual but rather to a hierarchy of individuals. Thus, he argues that the Marshallian entrepreneur is essentially "*an organization* which comprises all of the people required to perform entrepreneurial functions" (1956, p. 356). We find it difficult to reconcile this interpretation with the idea of the entrepreneur as a person of unique abilities who receives a quasi-rent, insofar as quasi-rents can only be ascertained for individuals, and any aggregation of these magnitudes seems specious at best.

Despite the fact that Marshall wrote during the high tide of competitive capitalism, his theory of entrepreneurship gave little prominence to invention and innovation (Shove 1942). Also, despite his lip service to evolution as a vital force in economics, he devoted his intellectual energies mainly to advancing the theory of comparative statics and partial equilibrium. For the most part, his students and disciples followed suit.

Francis Y. Edgeworth (1845–1926), a disciple of Marshall and an important neoclassical economist in his own right, recognized the importance of the entrepreneur, but added no new dimensions to the concept. In his first treatment of the topic, Edgeworth raised the proverbial question, "What is an entrepreneur?" (1925, Vol. I, p. 16). By way of answering, he reviewed the four "type-specimens" offered by (1) the classical economists (i.e., the entrepreneur as capitalist), (2) Francis Walker (i.e., the entrepreneur as noncapitalist employer), (3) Frederick Hawley (i.e., the entrepreneur as risk taker), and (4) Léon Walras (i.e., the entrepreneur who makes no profit).[4] Unfortunately, he neither reduced the list to a single definition, nor attempted a workable synthesis. Instead, Edgeworth suggested that the choice of definition is dictated by the ruling type of economic inquiry. But he registered his objection to the zero-profit entrepreneur, whether he be of Walras' or of Walker's construction.

Edgeworth returned to the issue of the zero-profit entrepreneur several years later, in a sustained attempt to defend Marshall's version of the entrepreneur against the "errors" of Walras. The real debate, however, was not about the action and significance of the entrepreneur; it was about the reward for the entrepreneur's effort. Edgeworth acknowledged Walras's contribution, but attacked his conclusion as paradoxical and unsound. In 1909 he wrote:

The central figure in the productive system is the entrepreneur. Buying the factors of production, the use of land, labor, machinery, and working them up into half-manufactured or finished products, which he sells to other entrepreneurs or consumers, at a price covering his expenses and remunerating his work and waiting. The symmetry of the entrepreneur with respect to the factors of production was first, I think, clearly enunciated by M. Leon Walras. (1925, Vol. II, p. 378)

The key to the above passage lies in the remuneration clause. Ostensibly, Edgeworth shared Walras' definition of the entrepreneur as a buyer of services and a seller of products. But he did not understand Walras' notion of profits. He speaks above of the entrepreneur's remuneration in terms of *wages* and *interest* (i.e., Marshallian profits).

Donald Walker (1986, pp. 17–18) has helped clarify the discrepancy between Marshallian profits and Walrasian profits. Walras (1926, pp. 225–26; 1965, Vol. II, p. 629) maintained that in equilibrium the entrepreneur would have no profit qua entrepreneur, but that he would have nonentrepreneurial income in the form of interest, rent, or (managerial) wages. Thus, Edgeworth's attack on the "paradoxical" notion of the zero-profit entrepreneur was based on a misunderstanding of the nature of Walrasian profits, and was therefore wide of the mark.

Finally, Edgeworth was unable to complete satisfactorily the analysis of income distribution by partitioning the entrepreneur from the other factors. "To determine at what point the capitalist ends and the entrepreneur begins," he wrote, "appears to defy analysis" (1925, Vol. I, p. 48).

Marshall's successor at Cambridge, A. C. Pigou (1877–1959) also took up the subject of the entrepreneur, but he was less interested in the theory of distribution than in the macroeconomic consequences of the entrepreneur's activities. From a microeconomic standpoint, his view of the entrepreneur was passive and unenlightening. He saw the entrepreneur as an owner and a broker, merely one link in the economic chain that connects production and distribution. "The entrepreneurs," he wrote, "by whom the stream of goods that comes to completion every year is legally owned, sell these goods for money to wholesale houses and shopkeepers" (1929, p. 132).

When he turned to the macroeconomy, however, Pigou spotlighted the element of uncertainty, which has an impact on industrial fluctuations through entrepreneurs' decisions:

Business men in making [production] forecasts are shadowed by immense uncertainties. . . . The immediate cause lying behind general movements of employment consists in shifts in the expectation of business men about future prospects, or, if we prefer a looser term, business confidence. (1949, p. 216)

British thinking on the subject of the entrepreneur developed little in the generation after Marshall, which came to be dominated by one of Marshall's most brilliant students, John Maynard Keynes (1883-1946). Keynes treated the entrepreneur rather perfunctorily, retaining some conceptual notions of the entrepreneur as financier and employer—the residual claimant of profit. Like Marshall, Keynes placed the entrepreneur in the role of decision maker within the individual firm. His function is to "fix the amount of employment at that level which [is] expectled] to maximize the excess of the proceeds over the factor costs" (1964, p. 25).

As an active factor of production, the entrepreneur must confront uncertainty in his attempts to forecast "effective demand." The significance of uncertainty in the Keynesian paradigm has generally been understated by all but a few of Keynes' disciples, yet in many respects it was his most revolutionary contribution. The well-worn story in the history of economic thought is that Keynes' concern with macroeconomic variables subsequently shifted economists' attention away from the entrepreneur toward the performance of certain aggregates in the economy. However true this may be, there is another side to *The General Theory*. Keynes' focus on uncertainty in decision making, and more generally on expectations, provides a link between Marshall's notion of "the entrepreneur as manager" and the contemporary theory of enterprise and radical uncertainty advanced, for example, by Shackle (see Chapter 9), a disciple of Keynes.

Be that as it may, Keynes' discussion of the animus behind entrepreneurial activity is distinctly uneconomic and must be approached with caution. His comment on the nature of the uncertainty faced by entrepreneurs is that "businessmen play a mixed game of skill and chance, the average results of which to the players are not known by those who take a hand" (1964, p. 150). This statement is innocuous enough, but in its wake Keynes did something extraordinary. He linked enterprise not to calculations of expected profit but to "animal spirits"—the spontaneous urge to action declared to be innate in the human psyche. Said Keynes:

It is safe to say that enterprise which depends on hopes stretching into the future benefits the community as a whole. But individual initiative will only be adequate when reasonable calculation is supplemented and supported by animal spirits, so that the thought of ultimate loss which overtakes pioneers, as experience undoubtedly tells us and them, is put aside as a healthy man puts aside the expectation of death. (1964, p. 161)

In the final analysis, Keynes' explanation of entrepreneurial activity rests as much on whim, sentiment, or chance as it does on rational expectations of profit opportunities. As such, it is an analytical dead end.

NOTES

1. The meaning of this statement, and its implications, are not quite clear. A counterbalancing tendency between gains and losses might be posited in a long-run analysis where all "projects" are lumped together (cf. Wieser 1927, p. 355). But from an individualist perspective, this assertion seems tantamount to the statement that each entrepreneurial opportunity has a 50–50 chance of success. Surely there is no a priori nor observed reason why this should be the case. In fact, Hawley and Clark later refuted this position (see Chapter 7).

2. We may now observe that the distinction which Walras made between "English" and "French" in listing his criticisms of past writers was somewhat artificial: Turgot was guilty of the same "error" as the English classical economists (i.e., not separating capitalist and entrepreneur); and Mill was guilty of the same "error" as Say (i.e., identifying entrepreneurship with the coordination and supervision of productive factors).

3. The noted Swedish economist, Knut Wicksell (1851–1926), offered a similar criticism. Wicksell (1893, p. 95) claimed that Walras' entrepreneur is a mere fiction, because: (a) the buying of services and selling of goods in which he supposedly engages is more apparent than real (i.e., involves mere exchanges of productive services against each

other); and (b) Walras completely overlooked the significance of time in production. Unhappily, in his own work Wicksell repeatedly blurred the distinctions between entrepreneur, landowner, capitalist, and worker.

4. On the respective theories of Walker and Hawley, see Chapter 7.

7   THE ENTREPRENEUR
       PARTITIONED

In essentials, the entrepreneur is a buyer of services and a seller of
their products.

H. J. Davenport

In this chapter, we turn our attention from Europe to the
United States. Although U.S. economics during the post–Civil
War period was mostly derivative, it nevertheless began to
assert its independence as the nineteenth century drew to a
close. Even before this newfound assertiveness, U.S. economics sustained a lively and ongoing interest in the place of
the entrepreneur within economic theory. From the outset,
U.S. economists improved upon the English treatment by
insisting that the entrepreneur be separated from the capitalist. Thomas Cochran (1968) contends that the early development of modern corporations in the United States may have
helped U.S. writers perceive entrepreneurship as a function
apart from that performed by the capitalist. In all likelihood,
this theoretic turn was also affected by a pervasive German
influence on U.S. scholars, many of whom received postgradu-
ate economics education in that country.

AMASA AND FRANCIS WALKER

As early as 1866, Amasa Walker (1799–1875) of Amherst College lamented the confusion in English political economy between the capitalist and the entrepreneur. Walker recognized the important role of the entrepreneur in creating economic wealth, but he did not range beyond production in his discussion of this special resource. He defined the entrepreneur simply as one who brings about "an advantageous union between labor and capital," and he identified this special agent, variously, as employer, manager, entrepreneur, projector, contractor, businessman, merchant, farmer, or "whatever else he may be called, whose services are indispensible" (1866, p. 279).[1] Although he called the reward of entrepreneurial effort "profit," Walker offered no real distinction between the reward to the entrepreneur and the return to labor. "Profits are merely *wages received by the employer* (entrepreneur)," declared Walker, and as such, they are regulated by supply and demand.

Ultimately, Walker traded one confusion (entrepreneur/ capitalist) for another (entrepreneur/worker). However, the following passage contains the barest glimmer of profit as a scarcity rent, an idea that his son, Francis Amasa Walker (1840–1897), later seized and expanded into a unique theory of profits:

If there are more laborers than are wanted, wages fall; if fewer they advance: just so with employers, or business undertakers. If there are too many competing for profits, the rate will fall until the excess is driven back into the ranks of labor. As there are, however, comparatively few, in proportion to the whole number of persons capable of labor, who have the requisite capacity and training required for transacting business successfully, and fewer still who can command the necessary means of capital, it will follow that the rewards of the employer will be larger than those of the persons employed. (1866, p. 285)

Francis A. Walker emphasized the fact that the entrepreneur, as distinct from the capitalist, is the chief agent of production. Like his father, he depicted the entrepreneur as an employer of other factors. Declaring that French economists since Say had been on the right track, he criticized other English and U.S. economists who depict the capitalist as the employer of labor, merely by the fact that he possesses capital. Walker's clearest description of the entrepreneur's function is contained in *The Wages Question*, where he declared that the entrepreneur's role is:

[T]o furnish technical skills, commercial knowledge, and powers of administration; to assume responsibilities and provide against contingencies; to shape and direct production, and to organize and control the industrial machine (1876, p. 245)

Walker allied himself with the French economists in terms of his theory of income distribution (1884, p. 203), but he also declared its affinity with Marshall's theory (1887, p. 275). Walker maintained that profit is the return to the differential skill and talent of practicing entrepreneurs. In other words, it is in the nature of a rent. "The term wages cannot be applied thereto," Walker declared, "without inducing a wholly unnecessary and mischievous confusion of ideas, leading directly to false results" (1884, p. 204).

Walker noted that the successful conduct of business under free and active competition depends upon exceptional abilities or exceptional opportunities (the former dominated his thinking). These abilities are not equally distributed throughout mankind, just as land of equal fertility is not uniformly distributed over geographic space. Successful entrepreneurs have the power of foresight, a facility for organization and administration, unusual energy, and other leadership qualities— traits that are generally in short supply. By analogy, profit is due to differential ability, just as land rent is due to differential fertility (or differential location).

Walker extended the analogy between rents and profits by proffering a theoretical, no-profits stage of production. As-

suming a homogeneous supply of entrepreneurs sufficient to
meet demand and clearly demarcated from nonentrepreneurs,
Walker asserted that

Either this class would, by forming a combination and scrupulously ad-
hering to its terms and its spirit, create and maintain a monopoly price
for their services in conducting the business requiring to be done, which
is altogether improbable, or, else, they would, by competing among
themselves for the amount of business, bring down its rate to so low a
point that the remuneration of no one of this class would exceed what
he could earn for himself in other avocations. (1884, p. 207)

This "no-profits" stage of production, Walker asserted, is
directly analogous to the "no-rent" stage of land cultivation.
Consequently, he concluded that profits form no part of the
price of manufactured products, any more than rent constitutes a part of the price of agricultural commodities.

In reality, of course, the talents of entrepreneurs are not
uniformly distributed across populations. In conceding this
fact, Walker identified four levels of entrepreneurs, each level
graded by its degree of qualifications. "First," he said, "we
have those rarely-gifted persons . . . whose commercial deal-
ings have the air of magic; who have such power of foresight;
who are so resolute and firm in temper that apprehensions
and alarms and repeated shocks of disaster never cause them
to relax their hold or change their course; who have such
command over men that all with whom they have to do
acquire vigor from the contact." Next, in descending order,
is a class of high-ordered talent, persons of "natural mastery,
sagacious, prompt and resolute in their avocations"; followed
by those who do reasonably well in business, although more
by diligence than by genius; and finally, the ne'er-do-wells of
the "zero-profit" class, those "of checkered fortunes, sometimes doing well, but more often ill; men who are in business
because they have forced themselves into it under a mistaken
idea of their own abilities, perhaps encouraged by the partial-
ity of friends who have been willing to place in their hands

the agencies of production, or intrust them with commercial or banking capital" (1884, pp. 208-9).

Except for the different gradations of entrepreneurs, it should be noted that the view of profit as a return to differential abilities was not original with Walker. We have seen that Mangoldt sketched the outlines of the theory decades earlier. In fact, it is curious that Walker aligned himself with the French economists in this matter, insofar as his theory had a greater affinity with Mangoldt's, whose contribution was perhaps unknown to him.

FREDERICK HAWLEY AND JOHN BATES CLARK

Another U.S. economist who insisted on the functional separation of entrepreneur and capitalist was Frederick B. Hawley (1843-1929), whose background included the lumber business and cotton brokerage. Hawley was a keen student of classical economics, but he was also a fiercely independent thinker who made up his own mind on analytic issues. He was led to a study of entrepreneurship by his reaction to Böhm-Bawerk's theory of capital and interest. According to Hawley, it is impossible to understand why capital has a price unless "we study industrial phenomena from the undertaker's point of view" (1892, p. 281).

In a series of turn-of-the-century articles in the *Quarterly Journal of Economics*, Hawley unfolded a risk theory of profit that he set against Böhm-Bawerk's theory. He equated enterprise with risk taking, and characterized the entrepreneur as the great dynamic force of a capitalist economy. Stressing risk and uncertainty, Hawley ranked enterprise with land, labor, and capital as the four fundamental divisions of productive factors. To Hawley, risk and uncertainty were commonplace in the industrial system. He asserted that

There is . . . in all industrial undertakings in which capital is engaged, and in some also in which capital is not engaged, an element of risk

which the final consumer has to pay for. And the reason is this: that
everybody except the gambler—everybody, that is, engaged in industry—prefers a certainty to an uncertainty. (1892, p. 285)

Here again we find a bonding of entrepreneurship and uncertainty true to the Cantillon tradition. Although Hawley
was apparently unaware of Cantillon's performance, he echoed
the phrases of his predecessor. The special peculiarity of
every business risk, Hawley asserted, is nothing more than
"the uncertainty of how the selling price of an unsold product
will compare with the cost, or how the cost of an unfinished
product will compare with the selling price, if the latter has
been agreed upon" (1893, p. 464).[2] Insofar as he recognized
that some elements of cost could be fixed through insurance,
there is also a slight Benthamite strain to Hawley's argument.
But it was John Bates Clark (1847–1938) who made Hawley
aware of the distinction between insurable and noninsurable
risk.

Hawley's ideas on entrepreneurship were provocative
enough to spark a lively debate between himself and Clark,
who was the United States' preeminent economist at the turn
of the century. Clark acknowledged that Hawley and Mangoldt had successfully overturned a misconception of the
Austrian theorists by pointing out that "men do not hazard
their capital for an amount of annual gains that in a long
term of years will just offset their losses. They demand more
than this and they get it" (1892, p. 40). However, Clark re-
fused to concede that risk bearing was an entrepreneurial
activity. He argued, as Schumpeter also did at a later date,
that all risk is borne by the capitalist.

Clark used the term entrepreneur "in an unusually strict
sense, to designate the man who coordinates capital and labor
without in his own proper capacity furnishing either of them"
(1892, pp. 45–46). It was his view that "the entrepreneur, as
such, is empty-handed," a phrase evocative of Kirzner's "pure
and penniless entrepreneur" (see Chapter 9). In other words,

the entrepreneur cannot risk anything because he has nothing to risk.

In later works, Clark couched his discussion in terms of statics and dynamics, giving a role to the entrepreneur that inspired Schumpeter to an eventual new formulation. The static state in Clark's analysis consisted of a situation where demand, capital, and technology are given. Static conditions do change over time, however: populations grow, wants change, and improved production technologies are discovered and implemented. In other words, departures from static state equilibria are evolutionary. The mobility of labor and capital is requisite to the restoration of new, albeit temporary, equilibria.

Clark's entrepreneur is the human agent responsible for the coordination that restores the economy to an equilibrium position.[3] According to Clark, this coordinator may perform several functions:

He may, for example, both labor and furnish capital, and he may, further, perform a special coordinating function which is not labor, in the technical sense, and scarcely involves any continuous personal activity at all, but is essential for rendering labor and capital productive. We shall term [this] the function of the *entrepreneur*. (1907, pp. 82–83)

This notion of the entrepreneur as the dynamic force that moves the economy back to equilibrium after some disturbance is still very much alive in contemporary theory, but it was soon to be challenged by Schumpeter's assertion that the entrepreneur is the agent that causes disequilibrium in the first place.

On the related matter of insurance, Clark (1892) recognized the differences between insurable and noninsurable risks (which he termed "static" and "dynamic"), but he did not go so far as to integrate this distinction into a general theory that based profit on risk as well as dynamic change.

Hawley offered two rejoinders to Clark's criticism, one in 1893 and a summary statement seven years later designed to answer Clark and other critics who had joined the debate in the interim. In the second rejoinder Hawley advanced the view that "all individual incomes are composite, and that it is hard to imagine one that does not contain an element of profit and loss, as there is an element of uncertainty in the income of everybody" (1900, p. 78). In its time this was an unorthodox view, as it went against the prevailing tendency to compartmentalize distributional returns to factors of production. Yet it was particularly stimulating to academic economists who stubbornly resisted the idea that the theory of enterprise was a dark corner of economics that hid nothing of real importance.

HERBERT DAVENPORT AND FRANK TAUSSIG

The theme that engaged Hawley in the 1890s was picked up again by Knight in the 1920s and expanded into a fuller theory of risk, uncertainty and profit. But before Knight's harvest of economic theory, two other writers sowed the field. In a much neglected book entitled *The Economics of Enterprise* (1913), Herbert J. Davenport (1861–1931) unveiled the first carefully orchestrated and sustained attempt to understand economics from the point of view of the entrepreneur. Like his teacher, Thorstein Veblen, Davenport was considered something of a maverick and iconoclast. His book created a minor furor. Frank A. Fetter (1914, p. 555), a leading contemporary, denounced it as radical and unsound, which may account for its comparative neglect thereafter.

While Fetter ranted about Davenport's "riotous rhetoric" and offbeat examples, he failed utterly to confront the genuine uniqueness of the book—its concerted attempt to reorient economics from the entrepreneur's point of view.[4] Davenport held that economics consists of analyzing and explaining the actions of entrepreneurs. "We live in a society organized under competitive entrepreneur production," he declared, and on this axiomatic base, he attempted to reconstruct economic theory. The fact that he did not succeed totally does not lessen the value of his attempt.

The Economics of Enterprise is a general treatise, purporting to explain production and distribution as well as the roles of money and credit. Its province is competitive economics, the central characteristic of which is price, which both conforms to, and distinguishes, the competitive order. Davenport's analysis bears certain imprints of the Austrian School, such as methodological individualism, emphasis on causal sequences (1913, pp. 110–11), recognition of elements of time preference (1913, pp. 219–22), the significance of opportunity costs (1913, pp. 62–63), and the necessity of decision making under uncertainty (p. 74).

Regarding the pivotal figure in the competitive price regime—the entrepreneur—Davenport echoed Walras with his statement: "In essentials, the entrepreneur is a buyer of services and a seller of their products (1913, p. 140). He also proclaimed that "the entrepreneur is the independent, unemployed manager; the one who carries the risks and claims the gains of the enterprise" (1913, p. 67). Doing Cantillon one turn better, Davenport argued that the entrepreneur faces uncertain costs as well as uncertain sales prices. The entrepreneur's true costs are uncertain for various reasons (some exogenous), but chief among them is the indeterminacy of his opportunity costs. Rather than be frozen in inactivity by uncertainty, however, it is the nature of the entrepreneur to hazard a guess and to get on with it. Thus, the entrepreneur "estimates and surmises and hazards where he cannot know, and as a sort of general summary, setting many things over against many others, he decides upon his line of largest net advantage, making often not better than a rough guess, but none the less, a decision" (1913, p. 74).

Cantillon told us long ago that the entrepreneur adjusts supplies in line with demand. Davenport described the process in greater detail. He said that entrepreneurs adjust relative supplies, each by working out his individual cost computations, including opportunity costs. These costs are themselves the manifestation of the fundamental relations of demand and relative scarcity. Davenport makes it clear that the entrepreneur does not *determine* prices. However, it is necessary to study the causes of price from the entrepreneur point of view, he argued, because "it is through the entrepreneur process that the ultimate causes are forced to obtain expression in a competitive society" (1913, p. 109). This viewpoint puts him at odds with later writers such as Ronald Coase, Kenneth Arrow, and Oliver Williamson who take the existence of markets as a starting point and who theorize that, in an ideal world, the price system can and will do everything, with no need of entrepreneurship (see Chapter 10).

Davenport was careful always to distinguish between the man of science (e.g., the economist) and the man of action (e.g., the entrepreneur). Despite the subjective and uncertain nature of economic costs, Davenport (1913, pp. 74–75) asserted that the task of the entrepreneur is relatively simple. He makes decisions based on calculations as best he can, taking the imperfect nature of the information that confronts him. He does not concern himself with things he cannot change. He merely adjusts to them. To do otherwise would "waste his energies as an entrepreneur" and make of him a "mere scientist."

According to Davenport, the degree and direction of entrepreneurial activity are dictated by costs and by prospective demand. He does not suggest that the entrepreneur engages in anything like "creative destruction," to use Schumpeter's term (see Chapter 8). Rather, the entrepreneur's role is to oversee the competitive market process, which is made intelligible through the interaction of demand and supply. Davenport hinted at the pervasiveness of entrepreneurial activity while emphasizing the elements of direction and supervision. "In the main," he wrote, the price "process is captained by the entrepreneur, is guided and supervised by him, and worked out through him." Furthermore, "all employers of labor or of instrumental goods for hire are entrepreneurs, no matter whether the prospective product is to be offered for sale or not" (Davenport 1913, p. 139).

In the final analysis, Davenport's entrepreneur, like Walker's, is an employer of the other factors of production. His reward, in Davenport's view, should properly be considered a subcategory of wages. Strictly speaking, profit is neither a return to risk, nor a payment for the labor of superintendence. It is a payment for "entrepreneur labor":

[P]rofit stands as merely one form of the remuneration of labor and is thereby a subhead under the broader interpretation of the term wages. It points to gain without the intervention of an employer; it is, then, remuneration to the entrepreneur for entrepreneur activity as such. This profit goes, truly, to him who takes the risk, but does not, therefore, go as compensation for the risk or in proportion to it. (Davenport 1908, p. 98)

By denying risk bearing as an entrepreneurial activity, Davenport aligned himself with Clark. Yet he rejected Clark's marginal productivity theory of distribution on the grounds that it requires information that is unobtainable, even by the wisest entrepreneur.

[I]t is beyond the wisdom of any entrepreneur to make an accurate ascription of the efficiency for gain in any one of the business factors jointly engaged in his gain-seeking process; still more is it impossible to regard the remuneration which is accorded to any one of several factors, in its market rental or price, as precisely expressive of its gain-aiding efficiency. As much as the entrepreneur can do is to attribute to each factor a degree of serviceability for his ends commensurate with what he has to pay for it and to treat whatever is left as due to his own personal activity in the quest for gain. But this is crude in theory; his profit is partly due to the fact that he is able to make an intermediate good or agent signify more to him than he has to pay for it in wages or rent. (1913, p. 148)

Frank W. Taussig (1859–1940), of Harvard University, repeated Davenport's belief that profit is a subcategory of wages, but he also characterized the entrepreneur as a residual claimant, which explains the irregularity of his income (1915, p. 159). Taussig's entrepreneur guides and directs economic activity. He is a multifaceted individual, but above all, requires imagination and judgement (1915, p. 163). Differential abilities do exist and are unevenly distributed among businessmen, according to Taussig, but he insisted that Walker's "rent-theory" of profits cannot explain the fundamentals of profit, only the differences in profits among entrepreneurs (p. 175).[5]

Taussig flirted with the Schumpeterian notion of the innovative entrepreneur as the singular architect of economic progress. He wrote:

If changes in the arts were to cease, if competition were to work out its results perfectly, if prices were to conform closely to expenses of production, the managers of industry would receive nothing but wages,—wages determined in the same fashion as other payments for labor. But in a dynamic state—a state of unstable equilibrium, of transition, of advance—there is opportunity for businessmen to secure something more. By taking the lead in utilizing inventions or improving organization they make extra gains, which last so long as they succeed in holding the lead. Business profits, so considered, are ever vanishing, ever reappearing. They are the stimulus to improvement and the reward for improvement, tending to cease when once the improvement is fully applied.

Whether the term "business profits" should be thus limited is primarily a question of phraseology. . . . The large and conspicuous gains are in fact associated almost invariably with advances in the arts, with boldness and sagacity in exploiting new enterprises and new methods. (1915, pp. 84-85)

It is unlikely that Taussig had read Schumpeter's *Theory of Economic Development* before he wrote these words, for the book was available only in German until 1934. At any rate, he could not totally break the link between profits and wages in his own mind. Thus, he added:

None the less, this mode of sharply separating business profits from wages seems artificial. Even the routine conduct of established industries calls for judgment and administrative capacity, and so for the exercise of the same faculties that are more conspicuously and more profitably exercised under conditions of rapid progress. To separate even roughly the earnings of a successful business man into two parts—one wages, the other 'profits' in the sense of gains from progress—would seem to be quite impracticable. Looking over the whole varied range of earnings among those engaged in the business career, it is simplest to regard them all as returns to labor,—returns marked by many pecularities, among which the most striking are the risks and uncertainties, the wide range, the high gains from able pioneering. (1915, p. 85)

In the final analysis, Taussig held that although innovation is one of the activities that may be performed by the entrepreneur, it is not the only one, and probably not even the most important one. Rarely, he asserted, do the requisite business qualities and inventive traits reside in the same person (1915, p. 164).

FRANK KNIGHT

Of all the U.S. writers, however, the one to whom we owe the fullest and most careful examination of the role of the entrepreneur is Frank Knight (1885–1972), whose contribution was twofold. First, he provided a very useful emphasis on the distinction between insurable risks and noninsurable uncertainty. Second, he advanced a theory of profit that related this noninsurable uncertainty on the one hand to rapid economic change and on the other to differences in entrepreneurial ability. In so doing Knight established a meaningful synthesis of the Hawley-Clark formulations.

Knight charged that previous "risk theories" were ambiguous because they did not distinguish sufficiently between two very different kinds of risk. On the one hand, risk means a quantity capable of being measured, that is, the objective probability that an event will happen. Because this kind of risk can be shifted from the entrepreneur to another party by an insurance contract, it is not an uncertainty in any meaningful sense. On the other hand, "risk" is often taken to mean an unmeasurable unknown, such as the inability to predict consumer demand. Knight dubbed the latter "true" uncertainty and geared his theories of profit and entrepreneurship to its magnitude. The best summary statement of the theory comes from Knight himself:

[N]ot all "risks" necessarily give rise to profit, or loss. Many kinds can be *insured against*, which eliminates them as factors of uncertainty. . . . The essential point for profit theory is that insofar as it is possible to insure by any method against risk, the cost of carrying it is converted into a constant element of expense, and it ceases to be a cause of profit and loss.

The uncertainties which persist as causes of profit are those which are uninsurable because there is no objective measure of the probability of gain or loss. This is true especially of the prediction of demand. It not only cannot be foreseen accurately, but there is no basis for saying that the probability of its being of one sort rather than another is of a certain value—as we can compute the chance that a man will live to a certain age. Situations in regard to which business judgment must be exercised do not repeat themselves with sufficient conformity to type to make possible a computation of probability. (1951, pp. 119–20)

Modern practice has refined Knight's distinction in the following way. Things once considered uninsurable because of lack of a measurable probability distribution have, in fact, been insured (for example, Liberace's fingers, Streisand's voice, Dolly Parton's bosom). Recent literature therefore makes three distinctions where Knight made two. Risk refers to the situation where the probability distribution of possible outcomes is calculable and known. Uncertainty refers to a situation where the possible outcomes are listable but the probability distribution of outcomes is not known. Radical uncertainty refers to a situation in which the possible outcomes of a given event are unknown and unlistable (because they are infinite).

Nevertheless, Knight's contribution offered a new refinement of Cantillon's theory of the entrepreneur as the bearer of uncertainty, because it isolated the concept of uncertainty and sharpened its meaning. Knight also added elements of economic evolution to his theory of enterprise. He asserted that the mere presence of uncertainty transforms society into an "enterprise organization" that is characterized by specialization of functions. The function of the entrepreneur becomes paramount in this kind of organization. According to Knight,

Under the enterprise system, a special social class, the business men, direct economic activity; they are in the strict sense the producers, while the great mass of the population merely furnish them with productive services, placing their persons and their property at the disposal of this class; the entrepreneurs *also* guarantee to those who furnish productive services a fixed remuneration. (1921, p. 271)

This Knightian uncertainty is not easily compartmentalized, for it pervades all human decision making. But it helps establish a boundary between management and entrepreneurship. According to Knight (1921, p. 276), the function of manager does not in itself imply entrepreneurship, but a manager becomes an entrepreneur when his performance requires that he exercise judgment involving liability to error, and that a condition prerequisite to getting the other members of the firm to submit to his direction is his assumption of responsibility for the correctness of his judgements.

An interesting corollary of Knight's theory is that profit could not exist without error. Because entrepreneurial profit depends on whether an entrepreneur can make productive services yield more than the price fixed upon them by what other people think they can make them yield, its magnitude is therefore based on a margin of error in calculation by entrepreneurs and nonentrepreneurs who do not force the successful entrepreneurs to pay as much for productive services as they could be forced to pay. It is this margin of error in the faculty of judgement that constitutes the only true uncertainty in the workings of the competitive organization. Furthermore, it is this uncertainty that is borne by the true entrepreneur and explains profit in Knight's use of the term.

Knight commented on the separation of capitalist and entrepreneur, again falling back on the position taken centuries earlier by Cantillon. Both agreed that the entrepreneur may or may not be a capitalist—usually he must of necessity own some property, just as all property owners can hardly be freed from risk and responsibility. The point both writers stressed is that whether or not an entrepreneur owns capital, the essence of entrepreneurship is not to be found therein. As Knight emphasized, "the only 'risk' which leads to [entrepreneurial] profit is a unique uncertainty resulting from an exercise of ultimate responsibility which in its very nature cannot be insured nor capitalized nor salaried" (1921, p. 310).

The range of possible activities undertaken by Knight's entrepreneur are wide indeed. One interesting idea along these lines has been expressed recently by Donald Schon (1963, p. 84). Schon portrays the entrepreneur as a champion of new ideas and technologies, willing to "put himself on the line for an idea of doubtful success," accepting the risk of failure. He sees the entrepreneur as a kind of "broker" of new technologies, noting that "technological innovation requires leaps that cannot be justified before the fact by those charged with the task. So, there comes into being a man who takes the burden of risk on his shoulders without formal justification . . . , entrepreneurs without authority" (1976, p. 118).

Jay Forrester (1965), however, cautions that today's entrepreneur gets but one chance to succeed—a dubious assertion, but one seconded by Modesto Maidique (1980). Not all economists have found Knight's formulation appropriate. Fritz Redlich (1957) contends that Knight's theory is of no use to the historian of entrepreneurship because it offers no distinction between ownership and control, on the one hand, and management and decision making, on the other.

Despite the diversity of theories of entrepreneurship surveyed to this point, they all share the common point of view that entrepreneurial activity is a response to some exogenous force exerted on the market system. The first truly radical departure from this overweening perspective was taken by an economist who etched his name in the annals of economics by declaring the entrepreneur to be an endogenous factor and something of a mischief maker to boot. That person was Schumpeter, whose views on the entrepreneur are the subject of the next chapter.

NOTES

1. Schumpeter (1954, p. 519) labeled Walker's *Science of Wealth* (1866) "a representative performance of the 'non-American' line of United States economics," alluding perhaps to the German influence mentioned above.

2. Compare with Cantillon's vision, as portrayed by Hoselitz (1960, p. 240), that the entrepreneur is someone who buys at a certain cost price and sells at an uncertain sales price.

3. On the deficiencies of the argument that the entrepreneur is a mere coordinator, see Hawley (1900, pp. 84-89).

4. To quote Fetter on Davenport, "Peruna, as an example of harmful yet valued products, is administered in large doses; and burglars with their jimmies, and loose women with their flaunting appeals, appear so often that they make some chapters of this book appear like an evening at the uncensored movies" (1914, pp. 562-63). It is noteworthy that Irving Fisher, commenting on Davenport's earlier work, *Value and Distribution* (1908), recognized the "radical if not heretical" nature of that book, but warmly praised its practical side and declared his hearty assent.

5. This same criticism had been levelled unsuccessfully against Walker by S. M. Macvane (1887, pp. 9–11). Taussig took no notice of Macvane's critique, nor of Walker's response (1888, p. 282).

8 THE ENTREPRENEUR RECONSTITUTED

The entrepreneur is never the risk-bearer.

J. A. Schumpeter

With few exceptions, the writers surveyed in the previous chapters worked within the equilibrium tradition of main-stream economics. The Austrians and Frank Knight were exceptions because they were particularly interested in dis-equilibrium processes. In the main, however, neoclassical economics concentrated on end-states (i.e., solutions in which the effects of uncertainty have been expunged from consideration). Uncertainty in the sense of the incalculable has no meaning in this mainstream approach, because solu-tions to economic problems require that the actual and the calculable coincide. Deviations of one from the other, such as true uncertainty allows, cannot be fully accommodated with-in the equilibrium tradition. Thus, Maurice Dobb correctly asserted that "in a system of economic equilibrium the work of the entrepreneur cannot be qualitatively different from that of any other agent of production" (1937, p. 559).

A more generous functional theory of entrepreneurship must allow some potential within the analytic model for the entrepreneur to engage in decision making that alters the equilibrium position of the enterprise. Clark took tentative steps in this direction, but he did not complete the process. Both Clark and the main subject of this chapter, Joseph Schumpeter (1883-1950) were influenced to some extent by the German Historical School, a group of writers who were critical of received ecomomic doctrine, especially the English variant. Schumpeter, as we shall see, placed the innovative entrepreneur at the vortex of his theory of economic development. Almost all modern theories of entrepreneurship take their origin from Schumpeter.

THE GERMAN HISTORICAL SCHOOL

The development of economic thought in the late nineteenth and early twentieth centuries progressed differently in Germany than it did in England or the rest of the Continent. This was due in part to the influence on economic method of the German Historical School. The historicists believed that in order to understand man's economic behavior and the institutions that constrain it, economics must describe human motives and behavioral tendencies in psychologically realistic terms. This group of writers specifically rejected the individualistic underpinnings of English political economy and the notion that man is a "hedonistic atom" (Spengler and Allen 1960, pp. 500-524).

The founders of the German Historical School were Wilhelm Roscher (1817-1894), Karl Knies (1821-1898), and Bruno Hildebrand (1812-1878). It was their contention that a thorough analysis and complete understanding of historical data were prerequisites to a proper development of economic theory. Roscher showed an early interest in the concept of the entrepreneur by expounding Turgot's version of the theory. His *Grundlagen der Nationalöekonomie*, originally published in 1854, avoided altogether the term *profit*, representing the entrepreneur as a managerial laborer who owns and directs a business on his own responsibility. His income, besides interest and rent, is described by Roscher as basically a wage.

The second generation of historicists is represented best by Gustav Schmoller (1838–1917). Reacting against Ricardian doctrine, Schmoller amassed mountains of historical data in order to analyze actual economic behavior. From his examination of these data he discovered a unique central factor in all economic activity—the enterprising spirit, the *Unternehmer*, or entrepreneur. Schmoller's entrepreneur was a creative organizer and manager whose role was innovation and the initiation of new projects (Zrinyi 1962). He combined factors of production to yield either new products or new methods of production. Schmoller's entrepreneur possessed imagination and daring. He was a more distinctive force than Roscher's "superior laborer."

Schmoller's ideas were extended by third-generation historicists, Werner Sombart (1863–1941) and Max Weber (1864–1920). Sombart introduced a "new leader" who animates the entire economic system by creative innovations. This entrepreneur combined the powers of organization described by Schmoller with a personality and ability to elicit maximum productivity from individuals engaged in the productive process. Sombart painted the entrepreneur as a profit maximizer, whether he be a financier, manufacturer, or trader.

The German historicists characterized the entrepreneurial process as a breaking away from the old methods of production and the creation of new ones. This disequilibrating process was particularly emphasized by Weber. He sought to explain how a social system, as compared to an individual enterprise, could evolve from one stable form (perhaps under an authoritarian structure) to another type of system. Historically, he identified such changes with a charismatic leader, or entrepreneur-like person (Carlin 1956).

Like so many writers, Weber began his analysis of change with a stationary state construct:

We may . . . visualize an economic process which merely reproduces itself at constant rates; a given population, not changing in either numbers or age distribution. . . . The tasks (wants) of households are given and do not change. The ways of production and usances of commerce are optimal from the standpoint of the firm's interest and with respect to existing horizons and possibilities, hence do not change either, unless some datum changes or some chance event intrudes upon this world. (1930, p. 67)

In such a stationary society there is nothing that requires the activity traditionally associated with the entrepreneur. "No other than ordinary routine work has to be done in this stationary society," declared Weber, "either by workmen or managers" (1930, p. 67). Yet, inevitably, change occurs. Weber described a likely scenario.

Now at some time this leisureliness was suddenly destroyed, and often entirely without any essential change in form of organization. . . . What happened was, on the contrary, often no more than this: Some young men from one of the putting-out families went out into the country, carefully chose weavers from his employ, greatly increased the rigor of his supervision of their work, and thus turned them from peasants into laborers . . . he would begin to change his marketing methods . . . he began to introduce the principle of low prices and large turnover. There was repeated what everywhere and always is the result of such a process of rationalization: those who would not follow suit had to go out of business. The idyllic state collapsed under the pressure of a bitter competitive struggle. . . . (1930, p. 68)

From this context, the alteration described is driven by an entrepreneur type. The critical characteristics of Weber's successful entrepreneur are his religious imperatives, which make up what is called the Protestant ethic. In the final analysis, therefore, Weber's theory of social and economic change is, like Marx's, as much sociology as economics.

JOSEPH SCHUMPETER'S CONTRIBUTION

Schumpeter revealed his concept of the entrepreneur within the broader scope of a theory of economic development. To Schumpeter, development is a dynamic process, a disturbing of the economic status quo. He looked upon economic development not as a mere adjunct to the central body of orthodox economic theory, but as the basis for reinterpreting a vital process that had been crowded out of mainstream economic analysis by the static, general equilibrium approach. The entrepreneur is a key figure for Schumpeter because, quite simply, he is the *persona causa* of economic development.

Schumpeter combined ideas from Marx, Weber, and Walras along with insights from his Austrian forebears, Menger, Wieser, and his teacher, Böhm-Bawerk. Rather than slavishly imitate the work of others, he melded these elements into something uniquely his own. With Marx he shared the views that economic processes are organic and that change comes from *within* the economic system, not merely from without (Clark's view). He also admired the blend of sociology and economics that comprised the theories of Marx and Weber. From Walras he borrowed the notion of the entrepreneur, but in place of the phantom-like figure of Walras' general equilibrium system, Schumpeter substituted a living, breathing entrepreneur of mind and body. Reflecting the Austrian economists' interest in disequilibrium processes, Schumpeter made the entrepreneur the mechanism of economic change.

ENTREPRENEURS AND INNOVATION

To Schumpeter, competition involved mainly the dynamic innovations of the entrepreneur. This view is most clearly and completely set forth in his *Theory of Economic Development*, first published in 1911, and echoed in later works of 1939 and 1950. Schumpeter used the concept of equilibrium as

Weber used the stationary state—a theoretical construct, a point of departure. He coined a phrase to describe this equilibrium state, "the circular flow of economic life." Its chief characteristic is that economic life proceeds routinely on the basis of past experience; there are no forces evident for any change of the status quo. Schumpeter outlined the nature of production and distribution in the circular flow in the following passage:

[I]n every period only products which were produced in the previous period are consumed, and . . . only products which will be consumed in the following period are produced. Therefore workers and landlords always exchange their productive services for present consumption goods only, whether the former are employed directly or only indirectly in the production of consumption goods. There is no necessity for them to exchange their services of labor and land for future goods or for promises of future consumption goods or to apply for any "advances" of present consumption goods. It is simply a matter of exchange, and not of credit transactions. The element of time plays no part. All products are only products and nothing more. For the individual firm it is a matter of complete indifference whether it produces means of production or consumption goods. In both cases the product is paid for immediately and at its full value. (1934, pp. 42–43)

Within this system, the production function is invariant, although factor substitution is possible within the limits of known technological horizons. The only real function that must be performed in this state is "that of combining the two original factors of production, and this function is performed in every period mechanically as it were, of its own accord, without requiring a personal element distinguishable from superintendence and similar things" (1934, p. 45). In this artificial situation, the entrepreneur is a nonentity. "If we choose to call the manager or owner of a business 'entrepreneur'," wrote Schumpeter (1934, pp. 45–46), then he would be an entrepreneur of the kind described by Walras, "without special function and without income of a special kind."

For Schumpeter, the circular flow is a mere foil. The really relevant problem, he wrote in *Capitalism, Socialism and Democracy* (1950, p. 84), is not how capitalism administers existing structures, but how it creates and destroys them. This process—what Schumpeter called "creative destruction"—is the essence of economic development. In other words, development is a *disturbance* of the circular flow. It occurs in industrial and commercial life, not in consumption. It is a process defined by the carrying out of new combinations in production. It is accomplished by the entrepreneur.

Schumpeter reduced his theory to three elemental and corresponding pairs of opposites: (1) the circular flow (i.e., tendency toward equilibrium) on the one hand versus a change in economic routine or data on the other; (2) statics versus dynamics; (3) entrepreneurship versus management. The first pair consists of two real processes; the second, two theoretical apparatuses; the third, two distinct types of conduct. The theory maintained that the essential function of the entrepreneur is distinct from that of capitalist, landowner, laborer, inventor. According to Schumpeter, the entrepreneur may be any and all of these things, but if he is, it is by coincidence rather than by nature of function. Nor is the entrepreneurial function, in principle, connected with the possession of wealth, even though "the accidental fact of the possession of wealth constitutes a practical advantage" (1934, p. 101). Moreover, entrepreneurs do not form a social class, in the technical sense, although they come to be esteemed for their ability in a capitalist society.

Schumpeter admitted that the essential function of the entrepreneur is almost always mingled with other functions, hence the appeal of Marshall's definition of the entrepreneur as manager. But management, he asserted, does not elicit the truly distinctive role of the entrepreneur. "The function of superintendence in itself, constitutes no essential economic distinction," he declared (1934, p. 20). The function of making decisions is another matter, however. In Schumpeter's theory, the dynamic entrepreneur is the person who innovates, who makes 'new combinations' in production.

Schumpeter described innovation in several ways. Initially he spelled out the kinds of new combinations that underlie economic development. They encompass the following: (1) creation of a new good or new quality of good; (2) creation of a new method of production; (3) the opening of a new market; (4) the capture of a new source of supply; (5) a new organization of industry (e.g., creation or destruction of a monopoly). Over time, of course, the force of these new combinations dissipates, as the "new" becomes part of the "old" (circular flow). But this does not change the essence of the entrepreneurial function. According to Schumpeter, "everyone is an entrepreneur only when he actually 'carries out new combinations,' and loses that character as soon as he has built up his business, when he settles down to running it as other people run their businesses" (1934, p. 78).

Alternatively, Schumpeter defined innovation by means of the production function. The production function, he said, "describes the way in which quantity of product varies if quantities of factors vary. If, instead of quantities of factors, we vary the form of the function, we have an innovation" (1939, p. 62). Mere cost-reducing adaptations of knowledge lead only to new supply schedules of existing goods, however, so this kind of innovation must involve a new commodity, or one of higher quality. However, the knowledge undergirding the innovation need not be new, as Schumpeter recognized. On the contrary, it may be existing knowledge that has not been utilized before. According to Schumpeter,

[T]here never has been anytime when the store of scientific knowledge has yielded all it could in the way of industrial improvement, and, on the other hand, it is not the knowledge that matters, but the successful solution of the task *sui generis* of putting an untried method into practice—there may be, and often is, no scientific novelty involved at all, and even if it be involved, this does not make any difference to the nature of the process. (1928, p. 378)

In Schumpeter's theory, successful innovation requires an act of will, not of intellect. It depends, therefore, on leadership, not intelligence, and it should not be confused with invention. On this last point, Schumpeter was explicit:

To carry any improvement into effect is a task entirely different from the inventing of it, and a task, moreover, requiring entirely different kinds of aptitudes. Although entrepreneurs of course *may* be inventors just as they may be capitalists, they are inventors not by nature of their function but by coincidence and vice versa. Besides, the innovations which it is the function of entrepreneurs to carry out need not necessarily be any inventions at all. (1934, pp. 88-89)[1]

The leadership that constitutes innovation in the Schumpeterian system is disparate, not homogeneous. An aptitude for leadership stems in part from the use of knowledge, and knowledge has aspects of a public good. People of action who perceive and react to knowledge do so in various ways; each internalizes the public good in potentially a different way. The leader distances himself from the manager by virtue of his aptitude. According to Schumpeter, different aptitudes for the routine work of "static" management results merely in differential success at what *all* managers do, whereas different leadership aptitudes mean that "some are able to undertake uncertainties incident to what has not been done before; [indeed] . . . to overcome these difficulties incident to change of practice is the function of the entrepreneur" (1928, p. 380).[2]

ENTREPRENEURIAL PROFITS

Schumpeter's entrepreneurial function contrasts sharply with the managerial function described by Mill, but it has a modest affinity with Marshall's entrepreneur, who is also a leader and a person of creative imagination. Like Marshall, Schumpeter separated the entrepreneur's profits from the earnings of management. However, Schumpeter flatly rejected the idea of profit as a differential rent, insisting that profit not be confused with other factor returns. He argued that the "jumbling together of interest and profit," has historically caused much mischief in economics, leading many writers to the erroneous conclusion that profits are always tending "towards equalization . . . which does not exist at all in reality" (1934, p. 153).

Like Clark, whose theory of profits he judged nearest his own, Schumpeter argued that the very existence of entrepreneurial profits means that equilibrium has been disturbed. Although both profits and the entrepreneurial function disappear in "the circular flow of economic life," Schumpeter conceived economic reality as a dynamic process of churning from one equilibrium to the next. The real action (e.g., economic development) occurs in disequilibrium. Thus we have his claim: "Without development there is no profit, without profit no development" (1934, p. 154).

But what is the fundamental nature of profit? For Schumpeter, entrepreneurial profit is a residual, a surplus of revenue over costs. A surplus may arise either because an entrepreneur's new combination of existing resources lowers costs or raises values (e.g., through production of new products). Either way, the size of the surplus is related to the entrepreneur's productivity, but not in the same way as the returns of the other factors of production.

The paradox of profits in the Schumpeterian system is that they are simultaneously like and unlike other factor returns. Schumpeter explored the analogy between profits and wages and concluded that they are not the same:

Profit is . . . not wages, although the analogy is tempting. It is certainly not a simple residuum; it is the expression of the value of what the entrepreneur contributes to production in exactly the same sense that wages are the value expression of what the worker 'produces'. . . . However, while wages are determined according to the marginal productivity of labor, profit is a striking exception to this law: the problem of profit lies precisely in the fact that the laws of cost and of marginal productivity seem to exclude it. And what the 'marginal entrepreneur' receives is wholly a matter of indifference for the success of the others. Every rise in wages is diffused over all wages; one who has success as an entrepreneur has it alone at first. Wages are an element in price, profit is not in the same sense. The payment of wages is one of the brakes to production, profit is not. One might say of the latter, but with more right, what the classical economists asserted of rent of land, namely that it does not enter into the price of the products. (1934, p. 153)

Many earlier writers—from Cantillon to Hawley—had emphasized the connection between the entrepreneur's profit and risk. Schumpeter broke with this tradition by emphatically denying that profit is the return to risk. Risk falls on the capitalist, he argued, or on the owner of goods, not on the entrepreneur qua entrepreneur. Despite unusual will and energy, Schumpeter's entrepreneur is a person with no capital. On this issue, Schumpeter sided with Clark and departed from his mentor, Böhm-Bawerk, for whom the entrepreneur was clearly the capitalist, with no possibility of separation.

Schumpeter's profit theory has been roundly criticized by Kanbur (1980) for ignoring other forms of risk besides mere financial risk. Kanbur cites opportunity costs as an ingredient of entrepreneurial risk, especially for the entrepreneur who is not a capitalist. One kind of opportunity cost is the risk to reputation, of which Schumpeter said: "Even though he [the entrepreneur] may risk his reputation, the direct responsibility of failure never falls on him" (1934, p. 137). From the following passage, however, it is clear that Kanbur rejects this view:

The individual need not run the enterprise himself. Indeed, part of the uncertainty facing him may well arise from self-doubt as to his *ability* as entrepreneur. This uncertainty could be circumvented by lending his capital to somebody who could offer a better distribution of returns, while himself taking up employment in which he is less uncertain of his ability. Those who do not do so "risk their reputation," at least in relation to the safe alternative, as well as risking their capital. The two risks can indeed be separated out for conceptual or analytical purposes, not least because the opportunity cost of the capital will, in general, be different from the opportunity cost of entrepreneurial effort, and it is relative to these opportunity costs that gains and losses, and hence risks, have to be conceptualized. (1980, p. 493)

Kanbur (1979) finds the Cantillon-Knight formulation of entrepreneurship more amenable to the task of modeling entrepreneurial behavior, especially for the purpose of discovering the relationship between risk taking and the distribution of personal income.

Many years ago, however, Schumpeter defended his conception as historically legitimate and nonidiosyncratic. Thus he wrote in *The Theory of Economic Development*,

As it is the carrying out of new combinations that constitutes the entrepreneur, it is not necessary that he should be permanently connected with an individual firm; . . . our concept is narrower than the traditional one in that it does not include all heads of firms or managers or industrialists who may operate an established business. . . . Nevertheless I maintain that . . . [my] definition does no more than formulate with greater precision what the traditional doctrine really means to convey. In the first place our definition agrees with the usual one on the fundamental point of distinguishing between 'entrepreneurs' and 'capitalists'—irrespective of whether the latter are regarded as owners of money, claims to money, or material goods. . . . It also settles the question whether the ordinary shareholder as such is an entrepreneur, and disposes of the conception of the entrepreneur as risk bearer. (1934, p. 75)

Schumpeter's defense notwithstanding, other economists have chided him for his relative neglect of the topic of uncertainty in the theory of entrepreneurship. Andreas Papandreou, now a Greek head of state and socialist, argued decades ago that uncertainty is fundamental to the understanding and appreciation of the environment in which entrepreneurs break away from the routine. To compensate for the deficiency in Schumpeter's theory, Papandreou posited an alternative definition that makes uncertainty explicit: "The entrepreneur would be the one who carries out innovation under conditions of uncertainty and unpredictability" (1943, p. 23).

AFTERMATH

Schumpeter's influence on the theory of economic development has been enormous, even among those economists who reject the theory outright. Those who would modify the theory are forced to deal with it on its original terms. Over the long haul Schumpeter's vision and theoretical apparatus have proven more winsome to economists than Weber's. In part, this is undoubtedly because Schumpeter's theory does not depend on extraeconomic factors. Both thinkers advanced leadership theories of the entrepreneur. Whereas Weber conceived the innovator as an "ideal type" of the Protestant worldly ascetic, Schumpeter portrayed him as the supernormal economic agent. The latter is a more plausible analytic strategem, because in a theory of economic evolution it is more meaningful to postulate the appearance of someone of extraordinary economic ability as a mechanism of change than to postulate the appearance of a Calvin or a similar charismatic figure.

Ronan Macdonald (1971) has argued perceptively that insofar as theories of economic change go, Schumpeter's analysis occupies the middle ground between Marshall and Weber. Marshall's theory adapted incrementally to shifts in preference and production functions, the result being a continuous improvement in moral qualities, tastes, and economic techniques. Its shortcoming was that it did not explain business cycles, a deficiency that Marshall's student Keynes set about to remedy. Marshall's approach also implied a theory of uni-linear progress, which Schumpeter's theory denies. Weber's theory developed its own set of moral imperatives and used them to explain rapid social and economic transitions that punctuate long periods of historical continuity. Schumpeter postulated the continuous occurrence of innovations and waves of adaptation, simply because entrepreneurs are always present and are a force for change.

Ultimately, the appeal of Schumpeter's theory of economic development derives from its simplicity and its power. This simplicity and power is summed up in the Schumpeterian phrase, "The carrying out of new combinations we call 'enter-prise'; the individual whose function it is to carry them out we call 'entrepreneurs'" (1934, p. 74). Yet despite the impor-tance of Schumpeter's contribution to economic development, the larger dynamics of his theory have failed to penetrate deeply into conventional economic analysis. Economic his-torians have been quick to apply the Schumpeterian paradigm, however, as indicated at the beginning of this chapter.[3] On the pragmatic side, Albert Hirschman has tried to bolster Schumpeter's perspective by emphasizing a "cooperative" component of entrepreneurship in addition to the creative component. For Hirschman, an entrepreneur must be more than a creative "rebel," he must also embody "the ability to engineer agreement among all interested parties, such as the inventor of the [new] process, the partner, the capitalist, the supplier of parts and services, the distributors, etc." (1958, p. 17). Like many theories developed in the aftermath of Schumpeter's performance, however, this added perspective is a complement to, rather than a substitute for, the basic theory.

NOTES

1. The idea of entrepreneurship as innovation has had practical appli-cations as well as analytic impact. Sweeney (1985) contends that the

goal of the Six Countries Programme of growth in Europe is to promote innovation by supporting entrepreneurship rather than other mechanisms of growth (e.g., research).

2. Similar notions of the distribution of entrepreneurial talent on aspects of performance are in Brown and Atkinson (1981), and Acs and Audretsch (1986), who build on Lucas (1978).

3. For a recent example, see Hughes (1986).

9   THE ENTREPRENEUR
EXTENDED

The question of how the business man's mind works and what materials it works with in approaching a decision . . . is one of the most fascinating in the whole of economics.

G. L. S. Shackle

The essence of the entrepreneurial decision consists in *grasping* the knowledge that might otherwise remain unexploited.

I. M. Kirzner

Schumpeter's theory of economic development and the theory of entrepreneurship within it stimulated a new wave of research on entrepreneurship in the twentieth century. However, contemporary writers have reacted to Schumpeter in various ways. At Harvard University, Schumpeter's academic base of operations in the United States, a tradition emerged that espoused a particular methodological approach to defining the entrepreneur's role in the economy. This Harvard tradition approached the subject from the standpoint of economic history. Other writers have been more concerned with the analytics of Schumpeter's theory, especially the question of whether the entrepreneur is an equilibrating or disequilibrating force. Still other writers concerned with entrepreneurship divide themselves along neoclassical and Austrian lines. Our purpose here is not to reconcile all disparate approaches but to examine the different strands that have been woven into the fabric of contemporary economic theory.

HARVARD HISTORICAL STUDIES

In the wake of Schumpeter's treatment of economic development, a tradition of historical studies of entrepreneurship began at Harvard University's Research Center in Entrepreneurial History, established by A. H. Cole (1889–1974). Cole's interest in the entrepreneur and his views on the subject were influenced by E. F. Gay (1867–1946), founder of the Economic History Association and a follower of Schumpeter. The entrepreneur as a disequilibrating agent of change occupies a prominent place in Gay's philosophy of history, which asserts that the amount of permissable free competition existing in society varies with the social need. In this system of free competition the entrepreneur is a self-centered actor and a disruptive force, but according to Gay, "there are periods in the rhythm of history when . . . that disruptive, innovating energy is socially advantageous and must be given freer opportunity" (1923–24, p. 12).

Following Gay's lead, Cole emphasized the neglect of the entrepreneur by economic historians and by economic theorists. In order to discover the uniqueness of entrepreneurship and its importance to economics, Cole advocated a case study approach that employed various methods, including cross-sectional investigations of specific individuals over time, longitudinal studies of particular entrepreneurial functions (e.g., trends in personnel policies), and conceptual studies in historical entrepreneurship that might provide solutions to current problems.[1]

Cole's entrepreneur has two noteworthy features, each of which have early antecedents in economics. First, he is a productive agent who utilizes other productive factors for the creation of goods. Second, he makes decisions under uncertainty. In what was the most comprehensive (if not the most wordy) definition of entrepreneurship since Wieser, Cole proclaimed:

Entrepreneurship may be defined as the purposeful activity (including an integrated sequence of decisions) of an individual or group of associated individuals, undertaken to initiate, maintain, or aggrandize a profit-oriented business unit for the production or distribution of economic goods and services with pecuniary or other advantage the goal or measure of success, in interaction with (or within the conditions established by) the internal situation of the unit itself or with the economic, political, and social circumstances (institutions and practices) of a period which allows an appreciable measure of freedom of decision. (1949, p. 88)

"Purposeful activity" is potentially a multifarious concept. We take it to mean that entrepreneurial activity is directed toward some goal, presumably profit maximization. However, it may also refer to the rational ability to make decisions and to implement them.[2] "An integrated sequence of decisions" suggests the importance of organization in the conceptual understanding of entrepreneurship, a theme amplified by Leland Jenks.[3] The "business unit" as an institutional datum therefore constitutes the basis for a theory of entrepreneurial action in this view. According to Jenks:

Business unit and entrepreneur are interdependent conceptions. A business unit consists of a system of entrepreneurial and nonentrepreneurial roles structured as a system of exchange sets, productive performers, and cooperative activities. (1949, p. 151)

This passage illustrates a major theme of the Harvard economic historians, namely that the definition and meaning of entrepreneurship must be associated with environmental characteristics that influence the entrepreneur's decision-making process. In this, Cole and the others have followed Schumpeter's lead, since he perceived that the innovative actions of the entrepreneur impact upon the environment in a symbiotic fashion.

The interdependence of the entrepreneur and the business unit persists in many management-related academic studies. Thus, William Souder (1981) views research and development as one arena in which the entrepreneur guides and champions successful projects. Such individuals, "influenced by emotion and intuition," take risks by making "quick decisions" on a limited number of facts (1981, p. 18). In harmony with the Harvard theme, Souder suggests that many firms regrettably do not foster environments that encourage or enhance entrepreneurial activities. The reason is quite pragmatic: firms are engaged in active competition and accordingly tend to pursue conservative, proven approaches to new ventures.

SHACKLE'S ANTI-EQUILIBRIUM APPROACH

In a number of seminal works published over the last three decades, one writer in particular, G. L. S. Shackle, has focused his attention on the psychic act of decision in the world of enterprise. At an early point in his investigation of the nature and essence of business enterprise, Shackle (1955) identified two roles that must be performed. One is bearing uncertainty; the other is making decisions. These two roles are not unrelated because decision making involves improvisation or invention—actions that are genuinely possible only in a world of unknowns and uncertainties.

Shackle is at his best in explicating the nature of business decisions and the scope for human action within them. An astute Marshallian, he is critical of mainstream economic theory for its failure to recognize the full implications of time in the world of affairs. Shackle has been eloquent in his exposition of the essential problem with which time confronts economic analysis:

How to find a scheme of thought about the basic nature of human affairs, which will include *decision* in the meaning we give to this word in our unselfconscious, intuitive, instinctive attitude to life, where without examination or heart-searching we take it for granted that a responsibility lies upon us for our acts; that these acts are in a profound sense *creative, inceptive*, the source of *historical novelty*; that each such act is, as it were, the unconnected starting point of a new thread in the tapestry which time is weaving. (1966, p. 73)

Shackle's approach to entrepreneurship demands that uncertainty be faced squarely, and that deterministic models be rejected, but that some sort of order nevertheless holds in the world of practical affairs. In sum, his research agenda calls for the reconciliation of uncertainty and imaginative experience. These two elements comprise every business decision. But what is uncertainty? To Shackle uncertainty is a state of mind, something subjective. This subjective magnitude is nevertheless bounded by possibility, a condition required to keep the problem under investigation within the scope of analytic manipulation. Shackle explains the nature of bounded uncertainty along with the history-making activities of the entrepreneur:

If a man can set no bounds to what may follow upon any act of his own, he evidently looks upon himself as powerless to affect the course of events. There are, indeed, two views of history which would compel him to acknowledge his own powerlessness. If history is determinate, he cannot alter its predestinate course. If history is anarchy and randomness, he cannot modify this randomness nor mitigate the orderlessness of events. It is only a *bounded* uncertainty that will permit him to act creatively. (1966, p. 86)

To Shackle, uncertainty means plurality of rival hypotheses regarding outcomes of a given action. Each outcome is considered mutually exclusive, yet possible. Decision therefore means (1) the pursuit of imaginative experience, and (2) choice in the face of bounded uncertainty. Most of Shackle's work elaborates the second of these two elements. Eschewing the ambiguous term entrepreneur, Shackle calls decision makers "enterprisers." Although the motive behind this shift in terminology is plain, there is nevertheless strong kinship between Shackle's enterpriser and Cantillon's entrepreneur. This resemblance surfaces when Shackle specifies the nature of the enterpriser:

Uncertainty is inherent in production, but it does not follow that all who take part in it need bear uncertainty; those who wish can contract out of uncertainty. Let us assume that money is regarded by everyone as an unchanging standard of value. Then if, amongst all those who intend to contribute the services of themselves or of their property to the making of some exchangeable thing, some agree to accept from the others all their rights in the product, we can say that at the date when these contracts are made the planned operation has two quite different meanings for the two groups of producers. To one group it means an income of known size, for the other group it means the unknown difference between the total of the contractual payments and the price for which the product will exchange. Let us treat this second group as a single person and call him the enterpriser, and let us ascribe to him both of the two roles ... , that of decision-maker and that of uncertainty bearer. Then what induces him to venture on production is something essentially different in character from what induces the recipients of contractual incomes to furnish their services. (1955, pp. 82-83)

Demonstrating his affinity to Cantillon, Shackle pushes the analysis forward by attempting to get inside the entrepreneur's head, as it were, in order to discover the basis of enterprising decisions. His treatment of the subject evokes a combination of Marshallian, Keynesian and Austrian concerns. Like Marshall, he seeks to integrate fully the effects of time into the economics of decision making. Like Keynes, he confronts the matter of uncertainty. Like Menger et al., he is a radical subjectivist. Yet there are important differences, too. Unlike either of the above, Shackle's approach to economics is psychological and anti-equilibrium.

Shackle regards his own work as an extension of a Keynesian problem, namely, the determinants of business investment. He perceives a fundamental inconsistency in the Keynesian paradigm. He has called Keynes's *General Theory* "a paradox, for its central concern is with uncertainty, decisions based on conjecture, and situations altogether lacking in objective stability, yet it uses an equilibrium method" (1955, p. 222). In reaction to this anomaly, Shackle jettisons the equilibrium method—a radical stroke which probably accounts for the failure of mainstream economics to take him more seriously. Shackle's true followers are relatively few. The most prominent is Ludwig Lachmann, who also exhibits strong Austrian tendencies.

ENTREPRENEURSHIP AND HUMAN CAPITAL

An interesting extension of the theory of entrepreneurship fully within the neoclassical paradigm has been explicated by Nobel laureate T. W. Schultz, one of the pioneers of human-capital theory. Schultz finds in contemporary economic literature a persistent failure to see the rewards that accrue to those who bring about economic equilibration, especially as it occurs in certain nonmarket activities. Characteristically, Schultz approaches entrepreneurship from the standpoint of human capital. This view leads him to criticize the standard concept and treatment of entrepreneurship on mainly four grounds (1975, p. 832): (1) the concept is usually restricted to businessmen, (2) it does not take into account the differences in allocative abilities among entrepreneurs, (3) the supply of entrepreneurship is not treated as a scarce resource, and (4) entrepreneurship is neglected whenever general equilibrium considerations dominate economic inquiry.

Schultz's contribution consists of two major advances. First, he redefined the concept of entrepreneurship as "the ability to deal with disequilibria," and extended the notion to nonmarket activities (e.g., household decisions, allocation of time, etc.) as well as market activities. Second, he has brought evidence to bear on the effects of education on people's ability to perceive and react to disequilibria.

In his extension of the concept of entrepreneurship, Schultz argues, in effect, that Schumpeter did not go far enough in his formulation. "Whether or not economic growth is deemed to be 'progress'," declares Schultz (1975, p. 832), "it is a process beset with various classes of disequilibria." And whereas Schumpeter's entrepreneur "*creates* developmental disequilibria," his function is not extended successfully to "all manner of other disequilibria," including laborers who are reallocating their labor services, students, housewives, and consumers who are reallocating their resources, mainly time. Schultz (1980, p. 438) also contends that Schumpeter's entrepreneurs have become a decreasing part of the technological story in present-day society because of the growth of research and development in the public sector, a development that Schumpeter could not have anticipated. In point of fact, Schumpeter spent many pages in his *Capitalism, Socialism and Democracy* (3rd ed., 1950) explicitly lamenting the fact that the growth of bureaucracy *dampens* the pioneering and innovating spirit.

Unlike Shackle, Schultz has been an ardent defender of the equilibrium method. He has argued that

Unless we develop equilibrating models, the function of this particular ability [entrepreneurship] cannot be analyzed. Within such models, the function of entrepreneurship would be much extended and the supply of entrepreneurial ability would be treated as a scarce resource (1975, p. 843)

Schultz's theory of entrepreneurship attempts to discriminate between the disequilibria faced by firms, households, and individuals, so as to trace out supply functions for the useful ability to deal with disequilibria. Supply, in this sense, "depends upon the stock of a particular form of human capital at any point in time and on the costs and the rate at which the stock can be increased in response to the rewards derived from the services of these abilities" (1975, p. 834). Testing the effects of education in this connection, Schultz finds it to be a strong explanatory variable.[4]

At base, Schultz's approach to entrepreneurship is shaped by the dominance of the neoclassical paradigm in his thought. According to this paradigm, because entrepreneurial ability is a useful service, entrepreneurs must have an identifiable marginal product. Thus, there must be a "market" for the service in the sense of normal supply and demand functions. Schultz takes the Mangoldt-Marshall position that the value of entrepreneurial activity is a differential return to ability. The following passage provides a summary view of his position:

The substance of my argument is that disequilibria are inevitable in [a] dynamic economy. These disequilibria cannot be eliminated by law, by public policy, and surely not by rhetoric. A modern dynamic economy would fall apart were it not for the entrepreneurial actions of a wide array of human agents who reallocate their resources and thereby bring their part of the economy back into equilibrium. Every entrepreneurial decision to reallocate resources entails risk. What entrepreneurs do has an economic value. This value accrues to them as a rent, i.e., a rent which is a reward for their entrepreneurial performance. This reward is *earned.* Although this reward for the entrepreneurship of most human agents is small, in the aggregate in a dynamic economy it accounts for a substantial part of the increases in national income. The concealment of this part in the growth of national income implies that entrepreneurs have not received their due in economics. (1980, p. 443)

By raising the connection between entrepreneurship and education in an explicit fashion, Schultz admits to taking merely "the first step on what appears to be a long new road" (1975, p. 843). This new road is sure to contain many potholes and detours. At the most elemental level, for example, it is not clear what the precise connection is between education and knowledge. Following Hayek, Fritz Machlup argues that formal education is only one form of knowledge; knowledge is also gained experientially and at different rates by different individuals. Individuals can accrue knowledge from their day-to-day experiences, which "will normally induce reflection, interpretations, discoveries, and generalizations . . ." (1980, p. 179). More specifically, Machlup asserts that the cost of acquiring knowledge is related to differential abilities. Thus, he writes:

Some alert and quick-minded persons, by keeping their eyes and ears open for new facts and theories, discoveries and opportunities, perceive what normal people of lesser alertness and perceptiveness, would fail to notice. Hence new knowledge is available at little or no cost to those who are on the lookout, full of curiosity, and bright enough not to miss their chances. (1980, p. 179)

Should we, therefore, synthesize Schultz and Machlup to construe that entrepreneurial abilities stem from cognitive *and* experiential events? Investments in factual knowledge are clearly possible, but there may yet remain innate differences in individual capacities to receive and assimilate knowledge from their surroundings. If so, the human capital approach to entrepreneurship may ultimately rest on a genetic base.

One noteworthy feature of the human capital approach to entrepreneurship is that it rejects the idea of entrepreneurial rewards as a return to risk. Schultz maintains that although risk is omnipresent in a dynamic economy, there is no exclusive connection between risk and entrepreneurial activity. In his words, "the bearing of risk is not a unique attribute of entrepreneurs. Whereas entrepreneurs assume risk, there also are people who are not entrepreneurs who assume risk" (1980, p. 441). This view is, of course, definitionally based. Because Schultz chooses to define entrepreneurship as the ability to deal with disequilibria rather than the ability to deal with uncertainty, risk does not enter prominently into his concept. By contrast, definitions of entrepreneurship that are uncertainty-based cannot logically relegate risk to a position of little or no importance.

THE AUSTRIAN REVIVAL

Before the dark shadow of Hitler's Third Reich crept over the entire continent, a number of second-generation Austrian economists emigrated from Europe in the 1930s. Friedrich Hayek went to London. Ludwig von Mises (1881–1972) and Schumpeter, both of whom had been students of Böhm-Bawerk, came to America. Although Schumpeter quickly found an academic home in the United States, Mises had a difficult time. Eventually he joined the faculty at New York University under special arrangement. There he became the standard bearer of Austrian economics, reaching out intellectually to a small but capable group of students and followers.

Mises defined economics as the study of human action. Human action that is distinctly economic takes place in a market framework. And according to Mises, the nature of market activity is that it is an entrepreneurial process. Like Clark, Knight, and Schumpeter, who developed their theories by first introducing artificial constructs of the economy (i.e., the static state; the circular flow), and then hypothesizing how entrepreneurial activity alters these states, Mises built his theory upon the notion of "the evenly rotating economy." The evenly rotating economy represents a rigid picture of the world—a state of equilibrium characterized by the elimination of change in data and time, a world of perfect price stability where market prices and final prices coincide. In such a setting human behavior can be nothing more than involuntary response. According to Mises, "this system is not peopled with living men making choices and liable to error; it is a world of soulless unthinking automatons; it is not a human society, it is an ant hill" (1949, p. 249). Only when human action is viewed as "purposeful behavior," will change occur, because "action is change." The express purpose of the evenly rotating economy is merely to provide a point of departure for construction of a realistic theory.[5]

A fundamental aspect of Misesian human action is that it influences the future and is influenced by the future. Mises declared that "the outcome of action is always uncertain. Action is always speculation" (1949, p. 253). Thus, participants in the actual economy make choices and cope with the subsequent uncertainties of the future. In this context, "the term entrepreneur . . . means . . . acting man exclusively seen from the aspect of uncertainty inherent in every action" (1949, p. 254). It follows that in the evenly rotating system, no one is an entrepreneur; but in the actual economy, "every actor is always an entrepreneur" (1949, p. 253).

By this view, capitalists who lend their assets with less than perfect certainty of repayment are entrepreneurs (although this does not imply that entrepreneurs must be capitalists). So too, are farmers; in fact no proprietor of any factor of production is untouched by uncertainty. Laborers are also entrepreneurs because their wages are determined by uncertain market activities. What we have here is a logical extension of Cantillon's original view of the entrepreneur. Casting a wider net than Cantillon, Mises brought the landowners and laborers that Cantillon had excluded into the entrepreneurial fold. Mises generalized uncertainty to all market activity.

Like other writers before him, Mises examined the role of the entrepreneur in the context of the theory of income distribution. He distinguished between functional distribution and historical distribution, drawing attention to the entrepreneur in each, and exposing the ambiguity of the concept in its dual use:

Economics . . . always did and still does use the term "entrepreneur" in a sense other than that attached to it in the imaginary construction of functional distribution. It also calls entrepreneurs those who are especially eager to profit from adjusting production to the expected changes in conditions, those who have more initiative, more venturesomeness, and a quicker eye than the crowd, the pushing and promoting pioneers of economic improvement. This notion is narrower than the concept of an entrepreneur as used in the construction of functional distribution; it does not include many instances which the latter includes. It is awkward that the same term should be used to signify two different notions. It would have been more expedient to employ another term for this second notion—for instance, the term 'promoter.' (1949, pp. 254–55)

It is tempting to identify this economic agent of the second type with the Schumpeterian entrepreneur, especially in the following Misesian statement: "The driving force of the market, the element tending toward *unceasing innovation and improvement*, is provided by the restlessness of the promoter and his eagerness to make profits as large as possible" (1949, p. 255, emphasis added). Yet Mises was at pains to distinguish his conception of the entrepreneur from Schumpeter's. Referring to "the errors due to the confusion of entrepreneurial activity and technological innovation and improvement," Mises declared:

Changes in the data, especially in consumers' demand, may require adjustments which have no reference at all to technological innovations and improvements. . . . The business of the entrepreneur is not merely to experiment with new technological methods, but to select from the multitude of technologically feasible methods those which are best fit to supply the public in the cheapest way with the things they are asking for most urgently. Whether a new technological procedure is or is not fit for this purpose is to be provisionally decided by the entrepreneur and will be finally decided by the conduct of the buying public. (1951, p. 11)

Clearly, for Mises "the activities of the entrepreneur consist in making decisions" (1951, p. 12), and while decisions regarding innovation and technological improvement come under his purview, such decisions alone do not constitute an exhaustive set where the entrepreneur is concerned.

In the capitalist tradition of economic development, profit and loss are the carrot and stick of entrepreneurial activity. "It is the entrepreneurial decision," said Mises (1951, p. 21), "that creates either profit or loss," not capital itself, as Marx thought. Capital can be used in support of either good or bad (mistaken) ideas. If utilized in support of a good idea, profit results; if used to underwrite a bad idea, losses occur. According to Mises, "It is the mental acts, the mind of the entrepreneur, from which profits ultimately originate. Profit is a product of the mind, of success in anticipating the future state of the market" (1951, p. 21)

However one perceives the differences between Mises' theory of entrepreneurship and Schumpeter's, there appear to be no significant differences at all between Mises and Knight on the matter. Mises, of course, brought some traditional Austrian concerns to the discussion, but on practically every fundamental point dealing with the subject of entrepreneurship he comes across as a "Knightian." His precise intellectual debt to Knight remains, however, a matter of speculation.

The most provocative of the "new" theories of entrepreneurship from the Austrian camp has been put forward by Israel Kirzner, a former student of Mises. Kirzner defines the essence of entrepreneurship as alertness to profit opportunities. Acknowledging the combined influence of Mises and Hayek, Kirzner offers his theory as a halfway house between the "neoclassical" view of Schultz and the "radical" view of Shackle. He attributes his basic approach to entrepreneurship to three important ideas: (1) Mises' central vision of the market as an entrepreneurial process; (2) Hayek's vital insight that the marketplace engenders a learning process; and (3) the conviction that entrepreneurial activities are creative acts of discovery (1985, p. x).

Like Shackle, Kirzner is critical of mainstream economics

because it leaves no room for purposeful human action. But unlike Shackle, Kirzner does not wish to abandon the framework of economic equilibrium. For Kirzner, the role of the entrepreneur is to achieve the kind of adjustment necessary to move economic markets toward the equilibrium state. This crucial role is overlooked, he contends, by economic models that focus on equilibrium results rather than the process by which equilibrium is attained.

Following Mises, Kirzner maintains that mainstream neoclassical economics—as equilibrium analysis—defines "a state in which each decision correctly anticipates all other decisions" (1979a, p. 110); one in which decisions are made and actions taken by mere mechanical calculations; judgement has no place; each market participant makes decisions that merely adjust given means to suit a given end. By contrast, in the Misesian dynamic economy, knowledge is neither complete nor perfect, therefore markets are constantly in states of disequilibrium, and it is disequilibrium that gives scope to the entrepreneurial function.

In his earliest formulation of entrepreneurship, Kirzner gave the impression of departing from Mises in several ways, thereby drawing the fire of otherwise friendly critics. One objection has been leveled against Kirzner's "pure and peniless entrepreneur," that is, an entrepreneur who does not own any capital. The gist of the argument against it is that if one has nothing to lose, there is no sense in which he can be said to bear risk, which is the essence of Mises' concept of entrepreneurship. Mises wrote: "There is a simple rule of thumb to tell entrepreneurs from non-entrepreneurs. The entrepreneurs are those on whom the incidence of losses on the capital employed falls" (1951, p. 13). Independently of Mises, yet allegedly in the same tradition, Kirzner has argued that the essence of entrepreneurship is alertness to perceived profit opportunities and that the full implications of this notion have not been made explicit by Wieser or by Mises, in whose works the idea resides.

In his lectures Kirzner likes to stress the analogy that the entrepreneur is a person who, upon seeing a $10 bill on the ground in front of him, is alert to the opportunity and quickly grabs it. The alert person will seize it rapidly; the less alert will take longer to recognize the opportunity and to act on it. Not all entrepreneurs are created equal. By stressing pure alertness in this fashion, Kirzner emphasizes the quality of perception, recognizing an opportunity that is a sure thing; whereas in reality every profit opportunity is uncertain. Kirzner's best known case for illustrating alertness is that of the arbitrageur, the person who discovers the opportunity to buy at low prices and sell the same items at high prices, because of differences in intertemporal or interspatial demands. In these cases, Kirzner's entrepreneur requires neither capital, as does Mises's entrepreneur, nor imagination, as does Shackle's enterpriser.

In response to several critics, Kirzner has elaborated his view of entrepreneurship vis-à-vis uncertainty. Lawrence White (1976) and Murray Rothbard (1985)—in his endorsement of a discussion by Robert Hébert (1985)—questioned the role of uncertainty in Kirzner's view of the entrepreneur. The issue raised by these writers is that arbitrage deals with present, known opportunities to exploit price differences that exceed transactions/transfer costs over time or space, whereas uncertainty exists solely with respect to the future. By confining entrepreneurial activity to the practice of arbitrage, therefore, Kirzner downplays the importance of uncertainty in human decision making. The consequences are important to economic analysis because a theory that ignores uncertainty cannot explain entrepreneurial losses, only entrepreneurial gains.[6]

Kirzner has recently confronted this asymmetry and has altered his position somewhat. He now contends that uncertainty *is* central to the notion of entrepreneurial activity but the relationship is more subtle than formerly supposed. Entrepreneurship that is also arbitrageurship involves discovery of past error (i.e., a single-period market decision), whereas entrepreneurship in the face of uncertainty involves multi-period market decisions requiring the imagination and creativity of the Shacklean enterpriser. Both views define profit opportunities, but the latter gives wider scope to the framework-constructing talents of the entrepreneur and therefore emphasizes his history-making role. The former view, by contrast, emphasizes calculation and judgement by the entrepreneur within a *given* framework.

In other words, Kirzner now defends a synthetic view of entrepreneurship that combines the epoch-making activities of the entrepreneur (à la Shackle) with the corrective adjustments of the arbitrageur, which he formerly stressed. In this new form, the nature of entrepreneurship is more directly traced backwards through Mises to the original formulation of Cantillon. Time and uncertainty may alter the form of action called entrepreneurship but they do not change its essential function. This realization is the basis for Kirzner's "wider view":

In the single-period case alertness can at best discover hitherto overlooked current facts. In the multiperiod case entrepreneurial alertness must include the entrepreneur's perception of the way in which creative and imaginative action may vitally shape the kind of transactions that will be entered into in future market periods. (1985, pp. 63–64)

In other words, one must specify the nature of the market process under investigation in order to understand the concrete manifestation of the entrepreneurial function within that process.[7]

The notion of a normal supply curve of entrepreneurial ability has become a major issue of contention between Kirzner and Schultz. Schultz (1980, p. 439) has criticized Kirzner for neglecting entrepreneurship as a scarce resource (i.e., failure to treat it in terms of a supply curve). Kirzner's response is that it is simply not useful to do so, because alertness involves no identifiable costs or required amounts (1985, p. 89). So far there has been no rapprochement on this issue because the two contestants have been at cross purposes. Schultz conceives entrepreneurial ability as a service—which, if it can be narrowly defined, may be amenable to the notion of a schedule of prices and quantities.[8] However, Kirzner regards alertness (i.e., entrepreneurship) as a human characteristic which is either present or not. For Kirzner, alertness, like beauty, cannot be fundamentally augmented once nature has dealt each of us our individual endowment.

Despite this fundamental disagreement, the theories of Kirzner and Schultz touch on a number of important points. Both writers view the entrepreneur as someone who perceives the opportunity for gain in a disequilibrium situation and acts accordingly. Both believe that the concept is all-important and much more extensive in scope than it has heretofore been represented in economic literature. The lines of demarcation between the two theories tend to be drawn on methodological rather than analytical grounds.

ENTREPRENEURSHIP AND X-INEFFICIENCY

Austrian economists like Kirzner offer a theoretical alternative to the general equilibrium paradigm of neoclassical economics. Their framework eschews the comparative-statics, perfect-markets vision of economic activity in favor of a system that emphasizes change, error, and imperfections in markets and in human decision making. Yet theirs is not the only challenge to the dominant paradigm, for we have seen that Clark, Schumpeter, and Shackle have all launched criticisms and alternative visions of the neoclassical framework that have met with some success. Another recent challenge that has come from outside the Austrian circle is the theory of X-efficiency devised by Harvey Leibenstein.

It is debatable whether entrepreneurship is central to Leibenstein's theory or incidental to it. What is clear is that the X-efficiency paradigm excludes precisely those aspects of the neoclassical framework that virtually eliminated the role of the entrepreneur. In a perfectly competitive world of general equilibrium, all participants are viewed as successful maximizers of utility and all firms are seen as producing efficiently. Leibenstein rejects this vision, substituting inefficiency as the norm. The market imperfections that account for X-inefficiency in Leibenstein's (1979) theory arise chiefly from organizational entropy, human inertia, incomplete contracts between economic agents, and conflicting agent-principal interests. In the X-inefficient world, firms do not necessarily maximize profits, nor do they always minimize costs. Obviously, one's view of what the entrepreneur does depends on his vision of the market. The X-inefficient world is one of persistent slack, which implies the existence of entrepreneurial opportunities. According to Leibenstein (1968), these opportunities fall into four categories: the connection of different markets, correction of market deficiencies (gap filling), completion of inputs, and creation or extension of time-binding, input-transforming entities (that is, firms). But Leibenstein's entrepreneur must work hard to discover such opportunities. The existence of slack and the fact that not all inputs are marketed tend to obscure profit signals, so that they must be ferreted out. A world with as many market imperfections as Leibenstein's must nevertheless give as wide a scope for entrepreneurial activity as a perfectly competitive situation takes away from it.

Leibenstein emphasizes the input-completing function as the critical role of the entrepreneur. This involves filling gaps in the production process and overcoming obstacles to production. Leibenstein asserts that "there are both empty spaces and fuzzy areas between what is being bought, and what can be done for productive purposes with what is bought" (1979, p. 134).[9] The one input that is always missing in Leibenstein's view is motivation. He views individual effort as a variable in production, and because of this, denies the existence of a unique production function. This last fact adds a dimension of entrepreneurial uncertainty that is augmented by organizational entropy within the firm, which the entrepreneur must try to overcome. Despite multiple responsibilities, however, input completion is the chief task of the entrepreneur in Leibenstein's paradigm:

Another way of looking at this matter is to say that the product space is not continuous. It is not so dense everywhere that every variety of product exists. Products come in discontinuous chunks, as it were, and not as individual characteristics or qualities. Hence the entrepreneur has to marshal enough of the missing or difficult to get inputs to produce an integrated collection of qualities. (1979, p. 135)

Leibenstein's vision leads to an open-ended theory of profits. In answer to the question what do entrepreneurs get, Leibenstein replies "whatever they can, or are clever enough to arrange to get." The X-inefficiency framework does not favor one theory of profit over another, it emphasizes a menu of contractual possibilities.

The nub of the matter is that the entrepreneur, as a consequence of his activities as an *input completer*, finds himself to be in a strategic position to work out (usually favorable) contracts, which determine in what form he is to receive his reward. . . . Some possibilities are the following: (1) He can become the residual claimant; or (2) he can be one of a group (for example, common stockholders) who are residual claimants; or (3) he can "forego" or sell his residual claimant reward and take a fixed share immediately of the capitalized value of the entreprise; or (4) he can appoint himself to a strategic managerial role in the enterprise so that he may receive both a wage and a share in the residual claims. (1979, p. 136)

Leibenstein's paradigm seems to touch the Austrian framework at a number of critical junctures, yet Austrian theorists have remained somewhat skeptical of its analytical potency. The tendency is for Austrians to interpret Leibenstein's entrepreneurship as merely one interesting feature of the ecnomic landscape, not as a factor central to the economic process. Kirzner has remarked that Leibenstein's entrepreneurship "is a feature that indeed seems to come into focus when observed through the X-efficiency lens; but the X-efficiency paradigm can be presented without any special reference to entrepreneurs" (1979b, p. 142). By contrast, in the Austrian framework, the entrepreneurial role is the key to understanding the entire course of economic phenomena. It is through the entrepreneur's thoughts and actions that what happens in the disequilibrium state is made intelligible.

NOTES

1. See also, Karl Deutsch (1949), who outlined a functional analysis of the study of entrepreneurship resembling Cole's. Deutsch proposed that the analyst first identify the single, most important technical or social function performed by the entrepreneur, then investigate this function (both primary and secondary effects) with respect to a particular time and place.

2. Hugh G. Aitken (1949) also stressed decision-making parameters in the entrepreneur's environment, such as advances in technical knowledge.

3. More recently, Minkes and Foxall (1980) have raised organizational issues in the study of entrepreneurship. Evans (1949), Spengler (1949) and Cole (1959) maintain that entrepreneurship is really a plural concept. Spengler has suggested that the entrepreneurial function can be conceived as a set of tasks that needs to be done and is done by an entrepreneurial group. See also Stauss (1944) and Schon (1976), who suggest that the firm be viewed as the entrepreneur, and Chapter 10.

4. In addition to works cited by Schultz (1975), especially Huffman (1974), see also Roberts and Wainer (1971), who conclude that a person's home and religious background as well as education have strong influences on goal orientation and motivation.

5. Mises defended the concept on methodological grounds: "There is no means of studying the complex phenomena of action other than first to abstract from change altogether, then to introduce an isolated

factor provoking change, and ultimately to analyze its effects under the assumption that other things remain equal" (1949, pp. 248-49).

6. Rothbard argues that even the arbitrageur is subject to uncertainty: "The arbitrageur can perceive that a product sells for one price at one place and at a higher price somewhere else, and therefore buy in the first place to sell in the second. But he better be cautious. The transactions are not instantaneous, and something might occur in the interim to change the seemingly certain profits into losses. It is, after all, possible that the other entrepreneurs, far from purblind to the profit opportunity lying await for arbitrage, knew something which our would-be arbitrageur does not" (1985, p. 282).

7. At least one study has given partial corroboration to Kirzner's theory. Patricia Braden (1977) concluded that the life histories of entrepreneurs in the state of Michigan demonstrated that their talents were founded not on their managerial abilities but on their capacities to recognize opportunities, that is, their alertness. In a related vein, following Usher (1954; 1955), Rossini and Bozeman define innovation as "mankind's striking response to the conjunction of resources and knowledge. [Innovation] is not only the seizing of emergent opportunities, but also a uniquely human response to perceived needs" (1977, p. 81).

8. While admitting the analytical intractability of entrepreneurship, Baumol (1983) has endorsed the notion of a supply curve of entrepreneurial ability based on a number of exogenous influences (e.g., genetics, cultural conditions, educational systems, attitudes toward economic success, etc.). Both Baumol and Schultz are squarely in the neoclassical tradition of economic theory.

9. Less hostile critics of Leibenstein maintain that the existence of "fuzzy areas" is characteristic of his theory as well, while more hostile antagonists question the very existence of the concept of X-inefficiency (for example, Stigler 1976).

10   THE ENTREPRENEUR AND THE FIRM

What has to be explained is why one integrating force (the entrepreneur) should substitute for another integrating force (the price mechanism). . . .

Ronald H. Coase

Economic theory and tradition present us with two basic explanations of why things are produced and distributed the way they are. On the one hand, the price mechanism is the allocator of resources, the integrative force in a market economy. On the other hand, the entrepreneur performs this function. The first economist to ask why one integrating force, the entrepreneur, should substitute for another, the price system, was Ronald Coase. In his pioneer article, "The Nature of the Firm," Coase (1937) questioned the paradoxical existence of *firms* as allocators of resources, when economic theory dictates that the price mechanism is an efficient allocator in competitive markets. If the competitive price system is an efficient allocator of resources, why do we have firms? And given that firms exist, does their presence imply either market failure or the absence of competition?[1]

TRANSACTION COSTS AND THE FIRM

In answering these questions, Coase applied the Marshallian notion of substitution-at-the-margin to his investigation of the internal workings of organizations. He asserted that firms exist because there are costs to using the price system that can be reduced or overcome by administrative arrangements. These costs are numerous and varied, but the most obvious to Coase was the cost of discovering what the relevant prices are. Contract and transaction costs for multiple exchanges make up most of the other costs identified by Coase.[2] In Coase's view, production can be organized through the price mechanism, an impersonal means of allocating resources, or through the administrative channels of a firm guided by a person or persons we shall call the entrepreneur.

Coase's theory of the firm offers an economic explanation for vertical integration. The entrepreneur's function within the firm is to detect where the costs of transferring resources from one stage of production to another via the price system (i.e., exchange) are high relative to the costs of transferring them via administrative act. "If an entrepreneur notices 'excessive' costs hindering the movement of resources from one stage to another, he internalizes the various stages of production so that they come under one roof of common ownership. This internalization economizes on transaction costs that would otherwise attend the transfer of resources from one stage of production to the next" (Boudreaux 1986, p. 18).

The limit to this kind of activity by the entrepreneur is determined by the costs of establishing and maintaining administrative arrangements that supplant the price mechanism. The costs of administrative direction rise with the size of the firm; that is, with the increasing number and complexity of administrative arrangements that comprise the institutional network of the firm. Thus, the efficient entrepreneur is always substituting at the margin. He increases the size of the firm whenever the costs of exchanging resources across lines of ownership exceed the costs of doing so by administrative action. He decreases the size of the firm whenever the costs of administrative transfer exceed the costs of market transfer. It follows that the entrepreneur's profit is equal to the cost saving achieved by changing the firm's size in line with the above principle.

In this view the firm is a true and literal substitute for the price mechanism because—as in general equilibrium price theory—the entrepreneur's task is pre-ordained. He is merely required to calculate administrative versus market costs and adjust his organization accordingly in line with the profit incentive. On close examination, the nature of decision making in this kind of firm involves neither human discretion nor uncertainty bearing. The chief merit of this view has been the illumination of transaction costs and how they affect the nature of the firm.

A "transaction costs" approach to the firm was pioneered independently by Arnold Plant (1937), who attempted to explain why firms become centralized or decentralized. Subsequent independent inquiries into organization theory by Edith Penrose (1959), Alfred Chandler (1962), and Harold Malmgren (1961) also extended the analysis initiated by Coase. Penrose theorized that firms evolve in a dynamic state of rivalrous competition as a consequence of the plans and wilful acts of entrepreneurs. The growth and prosperity of each firm, therefore, depends on the entrepreneur's ability to plan effectively and to devise efficient administrative mechanisms and hierarchies. Chandler advanced the thesis that a firm's administrative structure is primarily a function of its business strategy. The connection to entrepreneurship is that he regards business strategy as an entrepreneurial activity because it involves foresight, deliberation, planning and dealing with uncertainty.

Malmgren refined Coase's analysis by his thoughtful elaboration of the costs involved in using the price system to allocate resources. These costs are attributable primarily to market imperfections and uncertainty regarding input prices. Malmgren concluded that "the market operates between firms, but the entrepreneur is the planning and coordinating agent within the bounds of any one firm" (1961, p. 399). Unlike Coase, he introduced the specific issue of uncertainty, yet he confined uncertainty to input prices and quantities only. The final end of the production process for both Coase and Malmgren is taken as fixed, so that the entrepreneur's judgement in either case does not extend to the choice of which product to produce.

ENTREPRENEURS AND
OUTPUT-PRICE UNCERTAINTY

This last issue affords a point of contrast between theories of the firm advanced by Coase on the one hand and Knight (see Chapter 7) on the other. Coase's theory, like all theories that eschew uncertainty, focused on the *execution* of economic activity rather than its conception and planning. Knight concentrated on the latter, noting how the presence of uncertainty induces major changes in the organon of economic theory:

With uncertainty present, doing things, the actual execution of activity, becomes in a real sense a secondary part of life: the primary problem or function is deciding what to do and how to do it. In the first place, . . . the producer takes the responsibility of forecasting the consumers' wants. In the second place, the work of forecasting and at the same time a large part of the technological direction and control of production are still further concentrated upon a very narrow class of the producers, and we meet with a new ecomomic functionary, the entrepreneur. (1921, p. 268)

According to Knight, this rise of the entrepreneur class brings about major changes in the basic form of business organization. Internal organization of a business cannot be entrusted to chance or to mere mechanical formula in the face of uncertainty. Entrepreneurs are required to make discretionary decisions. Firms are compelled to recognize the disparity among individuals regarding intellect, judgment, and venturesomeness. The successful business must establish an organizational structure to promote successful decision making. It does so, according to Knight (1921, pp. 269-70), by encouraging the confident and venturesome to assume the risk which the doubtful and timid wish to avoid. In a phrase, entrepreneurs "insure" the latter group by guaranteeing them a specified income in return for a share of the enterprise's outcome.

In sum, the Knightian firm exists because the real world cannot meet all the conditions for competitive equilibrium dictated by economic theory. Knight held that the price system is effective in allocating resources among alternative uses but that it does not establish the *pattern* of alternative uses. This establishment of the pattern of alternative uses is an entrepreneurial function. Thus, the essence of entrepreneurship is *judgement*, born of uncertainty. "Any degree of effective exercise of judgment, or making decisions," Knight wrote, "is in a free society coupled with a corresponding degree of uncertainty-bearing, of taking the responsibility for those decisions" (1921, p. 271). This responsibility is expressed in the collateral guarantees of fixed remuneration given by the entrepreneur to resource suppliers.

In its basic form and content, Knight's theory of entrepreneurship is the logical extension of Cantillon's early and rich insight into how markets work (see Chapter 3). It is also a logical antecedent to Coase's theory. The opportunity for transactions to take place must exist before the cost of such transactions can be used to explain the nature of the firm. Coase's analysis takes for granted the primary question of what to produce. Insofar as it emphasizes calculation rather than judgement, it provides no meaningful way to distinguish the entrepreneur from other hired inputs. In other words, Coase worked within the confines of standard, neoclassical price theory. He adopted the static, general equilibrium method of analysis, which abstracts from time and uncertainty. As a theory of the firm, his analysis is imaginative and insightful. As a theory of the entrepreneur, however, it is limited in scope and substance.

Like Coase, Knight considered it anomalous that firms exist in a regime of perfect competition. To explain the anomaly, he drove economic analysis outside the standard neoclassical paradigm. In place of the perfect foresight hypothesized in static, general equilibrium models, he substituted entrepreneurial judgement. He made uncertainty the cornerstone of his theory, and adopted the same concept of uncertainty (refined to distinguish between insurable and uninsurable risks) used by Cantillon centuries earlier. This traditional perspective places uncertainty at the point of final consumer goods and services. One can hear the echo of Cantillon in the following passage by Knight:

[T]he main uncertainty which affects the entrepreneur is that connected with the sale price of his product. His position in the price system is typically that of a purchaser of productive services at present prices to convert into finished goods for sale at the prices prevailing when the operation is finished. There is no uncertainty as to the prices of the things he buys. He bears the technological uncertainty as to the amount of physical product he will secure, but the probable error in calculations of this sort is generally not large; the gamble is in the price factor in relation to the product. . . . The main immediate sources of uncertainty are the amount of supply to be expected from other producers and the consumers' wants and purchasing power. (1921 pp. 317–18)

In Knight's theory of the firm, as compared to Coase's, this output price uncertainty accounts for the unique nature of the firm. Transaction costs do not enter the picture at this stage of inquiry, because they are secondary to the originative acts of (1) deciding what goods are to be produced, and (2) establishing the appropriate administrative organization to do so. Whereas Coase took markets for granted, Knight was interested in the dynamic problem of how markets are created. He viewed the creation of markets as an entrepreneurial function. Prices allocate resources, but they do not create markets; entrepreneurs do. From Knight's perspective, therefore, the price system could never be viewed as a complete substitute for the entrepreneur.

Coase criticized Knight's theory of entrepreneurship because it neglected the role of contracts in defining entrepreneurial activity. However, we have seen that the chief function of Knight's entrepreneur is to contract away uncertainty by offering collateral guarantees of fixed payment to resource suppliers. Ironically, Coase found this element of contracting in Knight "irrelevant" (1937, p. 347). What mattered most to Coase was discovery of the reason why the price mechanism should be superseded, and he could not discover this reason in Knight's treatment of the firm.

Coase's perceptive analysis of transaction costs eventually spawned a new literature which takes perspective from the idea of the entrepreneur as contractor.[3] Thanks to Coase, the transactions cost literature has flowered in contemporary microeconomic theory. Nevertheless, his criticisms of Knight were mostly misplaced, because he did not understand the true nature of Knight's inquiry. Coase advanced the analysis of the firm within a neoclassical framework that accepts the choice of product as given. He therefore assumed away the uncertainty which Knight openly confronted. Coase argued that firms emerge because of the costs of using the price mechanism, costs that can be reduced or avoided by bringing more internal transactions within a single administrative network. As Boudreaux (1986, pp. 127–28) correctly asserts, however, this approach is more appropriate to questions of firm size (i.e., vertical integration) than to a theory of entrepreneurship.

Knight, like Schumpeter, was interested in explaining the nature of economic progress in a market system, the chief components of which are firms and entrepreneurs. By firm he meant a basic form of business organization in which the entrepreneur takes direction, control, and responsibility. Contracting alone does not capture the full role of the entrepreneur for Knight because "In the world as it is the interests affected by contracts are never all represented in the agreements" (1921, p. 353). In Knight's view, entrepreneurs are *more* than contractors. They are specialists at uncertainty bearing, and while the contract is one way to reduce uncertainty, some uncertainty can never be eliminated. For Knight, therefore, the size of firms depends, among other things, upon the available supply of entrepreneurial qualities (1921, p. 283).

IS THE FIRM THE ENTREPRENEUR?

Knight's theory offered a balanced perspective on the functions of risk taking and management. It set up a broad class of entrepreneurs because it did not limit the function of making provisional guaranties to the possessor(s) of the ownership equity in the firm. Indeed, one may have to move far up the management hierarchy in a Knightian firm in order to locate the function of ultimate control. Knight maintained that the primary function of management is the selection of people who make the decisions required by the operation of the firm. The basic structure of the decision-making organization is a hierarchy of functionaries in which persons at each higher level select the functionaries below. Therefore, each functionary leaves the consequences of his activity to his selector, thereby continually shifting economic responsibility to a higher level, until it finally rests with the controlling functionaries (i.e., the guarantors of the contractual remunerations of resource suppliers). For Knight, only this last decision is crucial; all subordinate decisions are routine, and consequently, nonentrepreneurial (1921, pp. 267–70, 276–77, 291–302).

In a forgotten paper published in 1944, James Stauss argued that Knight's theory, although logically correct, is neither the only solution to the problem of entrepreneurial control nor the most relevant one. Stauss claimed that the facts of modern business deny the concept of a unique class having primacy in undertaking the functions of risk taking and management. He proposed that the appropriate frame of reference for such undertakings is the firm. More specifically, he asserted that *the firm is the entrepreneur* (1944, pp. 112, 117, 120).

According to Stauss the central problem in a definition of entrepreneurship is determination of the locus of control. He found Knight's entrepreneurs not to be unique in this regard because

Primacy in exercising the function of control cannot be located formally in any one class of so-called "entrepreneurs" grouped on the basis of some other uniform relation to the firm (as possession of the ownership equity or extension of provisional guaranty). The circumstances of time and place demand consideration in locating the controllers and deciding upon the importance of their decisions. Likewise, decision-making within jurisdictional spheres is in the face of managerial problems of greater or less importance concerning the conduct of the firm. Cruciality of decisions is thus a relative matter. (1944, p. 118)

Stauss felt justified in his view by two developments of modern enterprise which he felt Knight neglected: (1) the rise of the corporation, in which the functions of ownership and decision making were largely separated; and (2) the expansion of government regulation, which tended to blur distinctions between ownership, regulation, and administration. Because of these developments, he argued that ownership was less important as a central relation of entrepreneurship than the decision-making apparatus, which normally resides in the administrative structure of the firm. Even in the case where the corporation is fully under private ownership, Stauss argued that "other governmental agencies, and various authorities, may dominate the policies of the firm in many respects, possibly to the extent of governing the selection of hired executives" (1944, p. 119).

Stauss claimed affinity with Schumpeter in terms of a shared view of the overall economic framework. This framework consists of an assembly of firms, supply functionaries, consumers, and government. Traditional theories of entrepreneurship (including Knight's), he maintained, confuse the actions of supply functionaries and some managerial laborers with the actions of entrepreneurs. However, if the traditional perspective is reversed so that the firm is the entrepreneur, then according to Stauss, "the functionaries introducing [Schumpeterian] new combinations would be, in the main, firms (old or new) acting through their aggregates of individual members with specified powers of decision" (1944, p. 121). The new frame of reference would be competent to analyze the basic responsibilities of laborers to yield productive services and to initiate and continue relations with the firm, including the productive services of managers that are not entrepreneurs.

Although it is provocative to think of the firm as the entrepreneur, certain questions are raised by reversing the traditional concept of the entrepreneur operating through the medium of the firm. Ultimately, humans, not structures, make decisions; therefore we must resolve the question of what is the firm? Other questions also crowd in quickly. What is the difference between a firm and a bureaucracy? Does firm size affect the origination and implementation of decisions? In short, how does the view that the firm is the entrepreneur improve the theory of entrepreneurship?

Successful firms tend to become larger firms, and larger firms tend to be dominated by rigid rules of conduct. The idea of the firm as the entrepreneur is likely to be opposed, therefore, on grounds of methodological individualism. Stauss rejected the notion that the firm is a mere aggregation of decision makers having a collective will expressed through a system of working rules. He proposed instead that the firm be treated as an accounting entity for purposes of general economic analysis, and as a peculiar, concrete institution when specific problems need to be solved (1944, p. 126). But he did not explain how this dual idea of the firm could be operationalized in economic theory.

After more than four decades, it is virtually impossible to find any trace of Stauss' influence on subsequent writers. The distinction between the entrepreneur and the firm, if there is one, remains blurred in contemporary economics, although the notion of personality apart from human beings is opposed in most quarters.

NOTES

1. Kenneth Arrow (1974) and Oliver Williamson (1975), among others, have argued that the existence of economic organizations *is* evidence of market failure.

2. For a detailed analysis of these costs, and of the effect of cost differentials on firm size, see Boudreaux (1986, pp. 18-30).

3. The classic reference to the "nexus of contracts" theory of the firm is Alchian and Demsetz (1972). See also, Jensen and Meckling (1976), Rubin (1978), Klein and Leffler (1981). More recently, Barzel (1987b) has used this approach to explore the moral hazard aspects of entrepreneurship. In a more fundamental historical sense, the idea of the entrepreneur as contractor harks back to Jeremy Bentham (see Chapter 5).

11 PAST, PRESENT, AND FUTURE

As the births of living creatures are ill-shapen, so are all Innovations, which are the births of time.

Francis Bacon

The preceding chapters explored the relationship between entrepreneurship and economics in historico-exegetic fashion. Our attention focused on writers who advanced the theory of entrepreneurship rather than on those who merely recognized the existence and function of the entrepreneur. The historical record reveals a diversity of opinion on the nature and role of the entrepreneur. Contemporary economic theory generally recognizes entrepreneurship as an independent factor of production on a more-or-less equal footing with land, labor, and capital. The distinction between manager and entrepreneur is now firmly drawn. However, the ultimate place of risk and uncertainty in the theory of entrepreneurship remains ambiguous, leaving profit theory in a kind of analytical limbo. The exact relationship between entrepreneurship and economic development is also a matter of ongoing debate.

A TAXONOMY OF ENTREPRENEURIAL THEORIES

Throughout intellectual history as we know it, the entrepreneur has worn many faces and played many roles. Neither economic theory nor economic history has fully defined his visage. Our survey identified at least twelve distinct themes that reside within economic literature:

1. The entrepreneur is the person who assumes the risk associated with uncertainty (e.g., Cantillon, Thünen, Mangoldt, Mill, Hawley, Knight, Mises, Cole, Shackle).

2. The entrepreneur is the person who supplies financial capital (e.g., Smith, Turgot, Böhm-Bawerk, Edgeworth, Pigou, Mises).

3. The entrepreneur is an innovator (e.g., Baudeau, Bentham, Thünen, Schmoller, Sombart, Weber, Schumpeter).

4. The entrepreneur is a decision maker (e.g., Cantillon, Menger, Marshall, Wieser, Amasa Walker, Francis Walker, Keynes, Mises, Shackle, Cole, Schultz).

5. The entrepreneur is an industrial leader (e.g., Say, Saint-Simon, Amasa Walker, Francis Walker, Marshall, Wieser, Sombart, Weber, Schumpeter).

6. The entrepreneur is a manager or superintendent (e.g., Say, Mill, Marshall, Menger).

7. The entrepreneur is an organizer and coordinator of economic resources (e.g., Say, Walras, Wieser, Schmoller, Sombart, Weber, Clark, Davenport, Schumpeter, Coase).

8. The entrepreneur is the owner of an enterprise (e.g., Quesnay, Wieser, Pigou, Hawley).

9. The entrepreneur is an employer of factors of production (e.g., Amasa Walker, Francis Walker, Wieser, Keynes).

10. The entrepreneur is a contractor (e.g., Bentham).

11. The entrepreneur is an arbitrageur (e.g., Cantillon, Walras, Kirzner).

12. The entrepreneur is an allocator of resources among alternative uses (e.g., Cantillon, Kirzner, Schultz).

Theories of entrepreneurship may be either static or dynamic. However, upon reflection, it becomes obvious that only dynamic theories of entrepreneurship have any significant operational meaning. In a static world there is neither change nor uncertainty. The entrepreneur's role in a static state could not be anything more than what is implied above in definitions 2, 6, 8, or 9. In a static world the entrepreneur is a passive element because his actions merely constitute repetitions of past procedures and techniques already learned and implemented. Only in a dynamic world does the entrepreneur become a robust figure. A dynamic environment is implied in definitions 1, 3, 4, 5, 7, 10, 11, and 12.

Once we have eliminated purely static representations of the subject, the taxonomy of entrepreneurial theories can be simplified by focusing on three major, intellectual traditions, each spawned by Cantillon. Broadly defined, these three lines of development are portrayed in the following graphic:

```
                    ┌─Knight-Schultz
    Cantillon ──────┼─Thünen-Schumpeter
                    └─Mises-Kirzner-(Shackle)
```

For purposes merely of identification, let us call these three traditions the Chicago Tradition (Knight-Schultz), the German Tradition (Thünen-Schumpeter), and the Austrian Tradition (Mises-Kirzner-Shackle).

This classification requires certain obiter dicta. To begin with, the lines of connection are not as straightforward as suggested by the graphic. Knight does not acknowledge Cantillon as the progenitor of his own theory of entrepreneurship, but the filiation of the two theories is too strong to ignore. Schultz (1980) openly aligns his theory with Knight's. The connection between Thünen and Schumpeter, however, is tenuous, as is the connection between Thünen and Cantillon. We base the linkage here more on convenience of exposition than on historical fact. On such grounds there is a certain logic of connection by the fact that Thünen was the first to exposit the entrepreneur as an innovator in a language shared by Schumpeter. Of the connection between Thünen and Cantillon, likewise, we have no direct evidence of linkage. There is no doubt, however, of the connection between Mises and Kirzner.[1] Shackle appears as a parenthetical entry with the Austrians because his basic concept of the entrepreneur is Austrian but he separates himself from them (and from all the writers in the graphic) by rejecting the equilibrium paradigm.

Despite its obvious oversimplifications, this classificatory scheme is useful for several purposes. It emphasizes, for example, that those writers who most advanced the subject of the entrepreneur did so in the context of economic dynamics, and the equilibrium paradigm.[2] Persistent themes in this literature emphasize perception, uncertainty, and innovation (or other special abilities). Some writers such as Schumpeter, assert that the entrepreneur creates disequilibrium, while others such as Kirzner, argue that he restores equilibrium after some exogenous shock. But this is a subtle difference which is of minor import to the overall understanding of the entrepreneurial function in a dynamic economy. Schumpeter certainly recognized the prevalence of other forces in the economy that work to restore equilibrium.

Another common theme among the above traditions is to regard the entrepreneur in functional terms, probably because functional theories in economics are heuristically more appealing than theories based on personalities. However, Schumpeter (1954, pp. 896–97) cited two reasons why a functional theory might not capture all of the entrepreneurial gains or losses known to business practice. In the first place, the entrepreneur who stands between the commodity and factor markets is better placed to exploit favorable situations—to capture certain "leftovers" or residuals. In the second place, whatever their nature in other respects, entrepreneurs' gains will practically always bear some relation to monopolistic pricing.

We find the first of these arguments more compelling than

the second, especially in view of Kirzner's (1973) attempt to clarify the distinction between competition and monopoly. By Kirzner's reasoning, true entrepreneurial gains have nothing to do with monopoly in its "proper" sense, which implies only that entry barriers exist. The problem of who has a legitimate claim to economic leftovers is, however, a thorny one that will, in our opinion, continue to plague the theory of entrepreneurship for some time to come.

TOWARD A SYNTHESIS

The hope that a historical survey of the conceptual nature of entrepreneurship might suggest a working definition of the entrepreneur that synthesizes the key ideas of past theories was a major motivation of this book. Having completed the survey, we propose a definition that bears a close resemblance to one recently offered by Mark Casson (1982). However, we believe that the aspects of uncertainty and responsibility must be made more explicit. We define the entrepreneur as *someone who specializes in taking responsibility for and making judgemental decisions that affect the location, the form, and the use of goods, resources, or institutions.*

This definition incorporates the ideas of risk, uncertainty, innovation, perception, and change. Like Casson, we hold that the entrepreneur is a person, not a team, committee, or organization. This person has a comparative advantage in decision making, and makes decisions that run counter to the conventional wisdom either because he/she has better information or a different perception of events and opportunities. Our definition implies that an entrepreneur must have the courage of his/her convictions and face the consequences of his/her actions, whether they produce profits or losses. Entrepreneurial activities, as Blaug (1986, p. 227) emphasizes, are performed in all societies by individuals whose judgement differs from the norm. Military and political life provide as much scope for entrepreneurship as economic life, but capitalism is a peculiar set of institutions and property relations that provides the widest berth for entrepreneurship.

Our definition accommodates a range of entrepreneurial activities within a market system, including: coordination, arbitrage, ownership, speculation, innovation, and resource allocation. It does not deny that entrepreneurship is typically mixed with other forms of economic activity, but it holds nevertheless that the essence of entrepreneurship can be conceptually isolated and separately analyzed.

Insofar as most past theories of entrepreneurship have centered on either uncertainty, innovation, or a combination of the two, it should be made clear that uncertainty is a consequence of change whereas innovation is a precept of change.[3] For this reason entrepreneurship emerges Janus-like from the annals of intellectual history. We see one face of entrepreneurship when the level of economic inquiry deals with the explanation of change and another when it treats the effects of change.

To illustrate this fact we recall one of the earliest stumbling blocks in the path of analytic advance on the subject of entrepreneurship—the inability or unwillingness of early writers to separate the role of entrepreneur from that of capitalist. True entrepreneurial gains, we now know, have no definite relation to the size of the capital employed in enterprise, but one thing that capitalist and entrepreneur have in common is that they face an element of risk. In the classical era, this commonality overshadowed small differences that were considered superficial. The chief social problem perceived by the classical economists was how to encourage the formation of capital that could be placed readily at the service of increased production.

Certaintly there were "capitalists"—those who accumulated wealth—in a feudal society, but they were not the merchant capitalists who rose to prominence in the seventeenth, eighteenth, and nineteenth centuries. These earlier capitalists were the landed aristocracy, whose capital was not "risked" in the production and sale of goods the way it is in an advanced market system. Recognition of this fact perhaps led Cantillon to exclude landowners from his class of entrepreneurs because they did not "live at uncertainty." The "new" capitalists of Smith's day were those adventurous people who took on large business risks in the hope of reaping great profits; their presence and central importance in society made recognition of a second group of risk takers (i.e., entrepreneurs) superfluous. Once capital was accumulated in the right hands, it was assumed that production would be organized and superintended by the selfsame person, and it was not deemed likely that the owner of capital would willingly give up its control and supervision; nor were there institutional factors encouraging him or her to do so until later. If this view seems shortsighted today, it is more the result of over 200 years of change in business practice than of a deficiency in the thought processes of our economic forebears. The fact is that the term capitalist was evolving into specialized use about the same time as the term entrepreneur, and for a time, at least, both meanings ran in the same channel.

This conjunction of terms might have persisted much longer had the focus of economic inquiry not switched dramatically near the end of the nineteenth century from economic development to income distribution. Investigation of the rewards for individual economic effort placed the differences between capitalist and entrepreneur in bold relief. It was then that perception, ingenuity, and judgement came to the fore as characteristics of the entrepreneur. But the new emphasis on income distribution was more or less coincident with the introduction of mathematical methods into economics. Such methods are analytically robust only within a static framework, which necessarily represses the role of the entrepreneur. Therefore, a paradigm shift that effectively highlighted the differences between the capitalist and the entrepreneur simultaneously suppressed the vital role of the entrepreneur as a force of change.

THE ULTIMATE DILEMMA

One lesson to be learned from all of this is that the problem of the place of entrepreneurship in economic theory is actually not a problem of theory. It is a problem of method. The history of economic theory clearly demonstrates that the entrepreneur was squeezed from economics when the discipline attempted to emulate the physical sciences by incorporating the mathematical method. Clearly, mathematics brought greater precision to economics, and thereby promised to increase its powers of *prediction*. Yet the introduction of mathematics to economics (about the time of Marshall) was a two-edged sword. Its sharp edge cut through a tangled confusion of real world complexity, making economics more tractable, and accelerating its theoretic advance. However, its blunt edge bludgeoned one of the fundamental forces of economic life—the entrepreneur. Since there was not then, and is not now, a satisfactory mathematics to deal with the dynamics of economic life, economic analysis gradually receded into the shadows of comparative statics, and the entrepreneur took on a purely passive, even useless, role.

Another historical lesson is that in its most fruitful phase, theorizing about entrepreneurship has been part of the search for the basic tenets of the dynamics of economic life. The dynamics of economic life involve relations between people as well as the relations of people to material things. As economics became more like a branch of mechanics, it struck a kind of Faustian bargain in which its "soul" was sacrificed for a better glimpse of the future (i.e., prediction). Yet this future should have been suspect all along, because the static method totally represses change. By contrast, dynamics *is* change, and more than anything else, change is the province of the entrepreneur.

Does it matter that the entrepreneur is the person who provokes change or merely adjusts to it? If we base our judgement on the most elemental features of entrepreneurship, the answer is, probably not. The basic features referred to are perception, courage, and action. Entrepreneurial action may mean creation of an opportunity as well as response to existing circumstances. Entrepreneurial action also implies that entrepreneurs have the courage to embrace risks in the face of uncertainty. The failure of perception, nerve, or action renders the entrepreneur ineffective. For this reason, we must look to these elements for the distinctive nature of the concept, not to the circumstances of action or reaction.

Just as theorizing about entrepreneurship has been most fruitful when economists have concerned themselves with the dynamics of economic life, so has it been least fruitful when economics has confined itself to the world of statics. At the close of our inquiry, therefore, we face the most basic of questions: What is the function of economics? Is it to enable us to understand the foundations of economic life, or to predict the course of events that have yet to happen? If it is the former, we must take economic life as it is, with its imperfections, its risks, its uncertainties. If it is the latter, we are justified in extruding from our theoretic models certain real life conditions, but we must become aware of the costs of doing so.

We are finally confronted with the ultimate dilemma. We may sacrifice realism on the one hand to gain precision, or we may give up precision on the other hand to gain realism. The choice we make determines the place of the entrepreneur in economic theory. Ultimately, the reason the entrepreneur is such an important subject of economists' interest is because his or her function and character penetrate to the very core of economics and raise fundamental questions of economic method that have never been resolved—indeed, have not even been fully discussed in the economic light of day.

NOTES

1. Cantillon appears to have influenced the Austrians through Menger, whose personal library (now permanently residing at the Hitotsubashi

University Library in Tokyo) contains a copy of Cantillon's *Essai sur la nature du commerce en général.* We are grateful to Professor Chuhei Sugiyama for providing us a catalog to the contents of the Menger Library.

2. Blaug (1986, p. 230n) reminds us that two decades after the publication of his *Theory of Economic Development* Schumpeter wrote a preface to the English translation in which he stated that the arguments of the book "might usefully be contrasted with the theory of [static] equilibrium, which explicitly or implicitly always has been and still is the center of traditional theory."

3. We do not deny that new methods and techniques themselves have consequences and that one of these consequences may be further innovation. Still, this does not deny the validity or relevance of our stated proposition.

BIBLIOGRAPHY

Acs, Zolton J. and David B. Audretsch. 1986. "Entrepreneurial strategy, entry deterrence, and the presence of small firms in manufacturing," Berlin: International Science Center (mimeograph).

Aitken, Hugh G. J. 1949. "The analysis of decisions." *Explorations in Entrepreneurial History* 1: 17-23.

Alchian, Armen A. and Harold Demsetz. 1972. "Production, information costs, and economic organization," *American Economic Review* 62: 777-95.

Aristotle. 1924. "The politics," translated by B. Jowett. In *Early economic thought*, edited by A. E. Monroe, pp. 3-29. Cambridge, MA: Harvard University Press.

Arrow, Kenneth J. 1974. *The limits of organization.* New York: W. W. Norton.

Barzel, Yoram. 1987a. "The entrepreneur's reward for self-policing," *Economic Inquiry* 25: 103-116.

————. 1987b. "Knight's 'moral hazard' theory of organization," *Economic Inquiry* 25: 117-120.

Baudeau, Nicolas. 1910 [originally 1767]. *Premiere introduction à la philosophie économique*, edited by A. Dubois. Paris: P. Geuthner.

Baumol, William J. 1983. "Towards operational models of entrepreneurship," in *Entrepreneurship*, ed. J. Ronen. Lexington, MA: D. C. Heath.

Bentham, Jeremy. 1952. *Jeremy Bentham's economic writings*, edited by W. Stark. London: Allen & Unwin.

———. 1962 [originally 1838-43]. *The works of Jeremy Bentham*, edited by John Bowring. New York: Russell & Russell.

Blaug, Mark. 1986. "Entrepreneurship before and after Schumpeter," in *Economic history and the history of economics*, ed. M. Blaug. Brighton, England: Wheatsheaf Books.

Boudreaux, Donald J. 1986. *Contracting, organization, and monetary instability: Studies in the theory of the firm.* Auburn, AL: Ph.D. dissertation, Auburn University.

Braden, Patricia L. 1977. *Technological entrepreneurship.* Ann Arbor, MI: Division of Research, University of Michigan.

Brandt, Steven C. 1983. *Entrepreneuring: The Ten Commandments for Building a Growth Company.* New York: New American Library.

Bronowski, Jacob. 1973. *The ascent of man.* Boston: Little, Brown.

Brown, D. J. and J. H. Atkinson. 1981. "Cash and share renting: An empirical test of the link between entrepreneurial ability and contractual choice," *Bell Journal of Economics* 12: 296-299.

Cantillon, Richard. 1931. *Essai sur la nature du commerce en général*, edited and translated by H. Higgs. London: Macmillan.

Carlin, Edward A. 1956. "Schumpeter's constructed type–the entrepreneur." *Kyklos* 9: 27-43.

Casson, Mark. 1982. *The entrepreneur. An economic theory.* Totowa, NJ: Barnes & Noble Books.

Chandler, Alfred D., Jr. 1962. *Strategy and structure.* Cambridge, MA: M.I.T. Press.

Clark, John Bates. 1892. "Insurance and business profits." *Quarterly Journal of Economics* 7: 45-54.

———. 1899. *The distribution of wealth.* London: Macmillan.

———. 1907. *Essentials of economic theory.* New York: Macmillan.

Coase, Ronald H. 1937. "The Nature of the Firm," *Economica*, N.S. 4: 386-405. Reprinted in *Readings in price theory*, edited by G. Stigler and K. Boulding. Homewood, IL: R. D. Irwin.

Cochran, Thomas C. 1968. "Entrepreneurship." *International Encyclopedia of the Social Sciences*, pp. 87-91. New York: Macmillan.

Cole, Arthur H. 1946. "An approach to the study of entrepreneurship: A tribute to Edwin F. Gay." *Journal of Economic History* 6: 1-15.

———. 1949. "Entrepreneurship and entrepreneurial history." In *Change and the entrepreneur*, prepared by the Research Center in Entrepreneurial History, pp. 85–107. Cambridge, MA: Harvard University Press.

——— . 1959. *Business enterprise in its social setting.* Cambridge, MA: Harvard University Press.

Davenport, Herbert. 1908. *Value and Distribution.* New York: Augustus M. Kelley (reprint 1964).

——— . 1913. *Economics of enterprise.* New York: Macmillan.

de Roover, Raymond. 1963a. "The organization of trade." In *The Cambridge economic history of Europe* III: 49–50.

——— . 1963b. "The scholastic attitude toward trade and entrepreneurship," *Explorations in Entrepreneurial History* 3: 76–87.

Destutt de Tracy, A. [1817]. *A treatise on political economy.* Translated by Thomas Jefferson. New York: Augustus M. Kelley, 1970.

Deutsch, Karl W. 1949. "A note on the history of entrepreneurship, innovation and decision-making." *Explorations in Entrepreneurial History* 1: 8–12.

Dobb, Maurice. 1937. "Entrepreneur." *Encyclopedia of the social sciences,* pp. 558–560. New York: Macmillan.

Drucker, Peter F. 1985. *Innovation and Entrepreneurship: Practices and Principles.* New York: Harper & Row.

Edgeworth, Francis Y. 1904. "The theory of distribution." *Quarterly Journal of Economics* 18: 159–219.

——— . 1925. "Application of the differential calculus to economics." In *Papers relating to political economy*, pp. 367–382. New York: Burt Franklin.

Ehrlich, Elizabeth. 1986. "America expects too much from its entrepreneurial heroes," *Business Week* (July 28): 33.

Euzent, Patricia J. and Thomas L. Martin. 1984. "Classical roots of the emerging theory of rent-seeking: The contribution of Jean-Baptiste Say," *History of Political Economy* 16: 255–262.

Evans, George H., Jr. 1949. "The entrepreneur and economic theory: An historical and analytical approach." *American Economic Review* 39: 336–355.

Fetter, Frank A. 1914. "Davenport's competitive economics," *Journal of Political Economy* 22: 550–565.

Fisher, Irving. 1908. "Davenport's value and distribution," *Journal of Political Economy* 16: 661–679.

Forrester, Jay W. 1965. "A new corporate design." *Industrial Management Review* 7: 5–18.

Galbraith, John Kenneth. 1967. *The new industrial state*. Boston: Houghton Mifflin.

Gay, Edwin F. 1923-24. "The rhythm of history." *Harvard Graduates' Magazine* 32: 1-16.

Gumpert, David E. 1986. "Stalking the entrepreneur," *Harvard Business Review* 64: 32-36.

Halévy, Elie. 1955. *The growth of philosophic radicalism*, translated by Mary Morris. Boston: Beacon Press.

Harbison, Frederick. 1956. "Entrepreneurial organization as a factor in economic development." *Quarterly Journal of Economics* 70: 364-379.

Hawley, Frederick B. 1982. "The fundamental error of *Kapital und Kapitalzins*." *Quarterly Journal of Economics* 6: 280-307.

──────. 1893. "The risk theory of profit." *Quarterly Journal of Economics* 7: 459-479.

──────. 1900. "Enterprise and profit." *Quarterly Journal of Economics* 15: 75-105.

Hayes, Robert H. and William J. Abernathy. 1980. "Managing our way to economic decline," *Harvard Business Review* 58: 67-77.

Hébert, Robert F. 1985. "Was Richard Cantillon an Austrian economist?" *Journal of Libertarian Studies* 7: 269-79.

Hennings, Klaus H. 1980. "The transition from classical to neoclassical economic theory: Hans von Mangoldt." *Kyklos* 33: 658-682.

Hermann, F. B. W. 1832. *Staatswirtschaftliche Untersuchungen über Vermögen: Wirthschaft, Produktivität der Arbeiten, Kapital, Preis, Gewinn, Einkommen und Verbrauch*. Munich: A. Weber.

Hirschman, Albert O. 1958. *The strategy of economic development*. New Haven, CT: Yale University Press.

Hisrich, Robert D. 1986. "Entrepreneurship and intrapreneurship: Methods for creating new companies that have an impact on the economic renaissance of an area," in *Entrepreneurship, intrapreneurship and venture capital*, ed. R. D. Hisrich. Lexington, MA: D. C. Heath.

Hoselitz, Bert F. 1960. "The early history of entrepreneurial theory." In *Essays in economic thought: Aristotle to Marshall*, edited by J. J. Spengler and W.R. Allen. Chicago: Rand McNally, pp. 234-258.

Hufeland, Gottlieb. 1815. *Neue Grundlegung der Staatswirthschaft-skunst*. Vienna: B. P. Bauer.

Huffman, Wallace E. 1974. "Decision making: The role of education," *American Journal of Agricultural Economics* 56: 85-97.

Hughes, Jonathan. 1986. *The vital few: The entrepreneur and American economic progress.* Oxford: Oxford University Press.

Hutchison, T. W. 1953. *A review of economic doctrines, 1870-1929.* Oxford: Clarendon Press.

Jaffé, W. 1980. "Walras' economics as others see it," *Journal of Economic Literature* 18: 528-549.

Jenks, Leland H. 1949. "Role structure of entrepreneurial personality." In *Change and the entrepreneur*, prepared by the Research Center in Entrepreneurial History. Cambirdge, MA: Harvard University Press, pp. 108-152.

Jensen, Michael and William Meckling. 1976. "The theory of the firm: Managerial behavior, agency costs and ownership structure," *Journal of Financial Economics* 3: 305-360.

Jevons, William S. 1931 [originally 1881]. "Richard Cantillon and the nationality of political economy." Reprinted in *Essai sur la nature du commerce en général*, by Richard Cantillon, edited by H. Higgs. London: Macmillan.

Kanbur, S. M. 1979. "Of risk taking and the personal distribution of income." *Journal of Political Economy* 87: 769-797.

———. 1980. "A note on risk taking, entrepreneurship, and Schumpeter." *History of Political Economy* 12: 489-498.

Keynes, John Maynard. 1964. *The general theory of employment, interest, and money.* New York: Harcourt, Brace and World.

Kiam, Victor. 1986. *Going for It!, How to Succeed as an Entrepreneur.* New York: William Morrow.

Kihlstrom, Richard E. and Jean-Jacques Laffront. 1979. "A general equilibrium entrepreneurial theory of firm formation based on risk aversion." *Journal of Political Economy* 89: 719-748.

Kilby, Peter. 1971. "Hunting the heffalump." In *Entrepreneurship and economic development*, edited by Peter Kilby. New York: Free Press, pp. 1-40.

Kirzner, Israel M. 1973. *Competition & entrepreneurship.* Chicago: University of Chicago Press.

———. 1979a. *Perception, opportunity, and profit: Studies in the theory of entrepreneurship.* Chicago: University of Chicago Press.

————. 1979b. "Comment: X-inefficiency, error, and the scope for entrepreneurship." In *Time, uncertainty and disequilibrium*, edited by Mario Rizzo. Lexington, MA: D. C. Heath.

————. 1985. *Discovery and the capitalist process.* Chicago: University of Chicago Press.

Klein, Benjamin and Keith Leffler. 1981. "The role of market forces in assuring contractual performance," *Journal of Political Economy* 89: 615-641.

Klein, Burton H. 1979. "The slowdown in productivity advances: A dynamic explanation," in *Technological innovation for a dynamic economy*, ed. C. T. Hill and J. M. Utterback. New York: Pergamon Press.

Knight, Frank H. 1921. *Risk, uncertainty and profit.* New York: Houghton Mifflin.

————. 1942. "Profits and entrepreneurial functions." *Journal of Economic History* 2: 126-132.

————. 1951. *The economic organization.* New York: Augustus M. Kelley.

Koestler, Arthur. 1959. *The sleepwalkers.* London: Macmillan.

Leibenstein, Harvey. 1968. "Entrepreneurship and development." *American Economic Review* 48: 72-83.

————. 1979. "The general X-efficiency paradigm and the role of the entrepreneur." In *Time, uncertainty and disequilibrium*, edited by Mario Rizzo. Lexington, MA: D. C. Heath.

Link, Albert N. 1987. *Technological change and productivity growth.* London: Harwood Academic Publishers.

Lucas, Robert E., Jr. 1978. "On the size distribution of business firms," *Bell Journal of Economics* 9: 508-523.

Macdonald, Ronan. 1971. "Schumpeter and Max Weber: Central visions and social theories." In *Entrepreneurship and economic development*, edited by Peter Kilby. New York: Free Press, pp. 71-94.

Machlup, Fritz. 1980. *Knowledge and knowledge production.* Princeton, NJ: Princeton University Press.

Macvane, S. M. 1887. "Business profits," *Quarterly Journal of Economics* 2: 1-36.

Maidique, Modesto A. 1980. "Entrepreneurs, champions, and technological innovation." *Sloan Management Review* 21: 59-76.

Malmgren, H. B. 1961. "Information, expectations and the theory of the firm," *Quarterly Journal of Economics* 75: 399-421.

Mangoldt, H. von. 1855. "The precise function of the entrepreneur and the true nature of entrepreneur's profit." In *Some readings in economics*, edited by F. M. Taylor. Ann Arbor, MI: George Wahr, 1907, pp. 34–49.

Marshall, Alfred. 1920a. *Principles of economics*. 8th ed. London: Macmillan.

———. 1920b. *Industry and Trade*. 3rd ed. London: Macmillan.

———. 1925. *Memorials of Alfred Marshall*, ed. A. C. Pigou. London: Macmillan.

Marshall, Alfred and Mary Paley Marshall. 1886. *Economics of industry*. London: Macmillan.

Martin, Dolores T. 1979. "Alternative views of Mengerian entrepreneurship." *History of Political Economy* 11: 271–285.

Mason, Edward S. 1931. "Saint-Simonism and the rationalisation of industry," *Quarterly Journal of Economics* 45: 640–683.

Meek, Ronald L. 1973. *Turgot on progress, sociology and economics*. Cambridge: Cambridge University Press.

Menger, Carl. 1950. *Principles of economics*, translated by J. Dingwall and B. F. Hoselitz. Glencoe, IL: Free Press.

Mettler, Ruben F. 1986. "Innovation, job creation, and competitiveness," in *The positive sum strategy: Harnessing technology for economic growth*. Washington, DC: National Academy Press.

Mill, John Stuart. 1965. *Principles of Political Economy*, edited by W. J. Ashley. New York: Augustus M. Kelley.

Minkes, A. L. and G. R. Foxall. 1980. "Entrepreneurship, strategy, and organization: Individual and organization in the behavior of the firm," *Strategic Management Journal* 1: 295–301.

Mises, Ludwig von. 1949. *Human action: A treatise on economics*. New Haven, CT: Yale University Press.

———. 1951. *Profit and loss*. South Holland, IL: Consumers-Producers Economic Service.

Morishima, Michio. 1977. *Walras' economics: A pure theory of capital and money*. Cambridge: Cambridge University Press.

———. 1980. "W. Jaffé on Leon Walras: A comment," *Journal of Economic Literature* 18: 550–558.

Neale, Walter C. 1957. "The market in theory and history." In *Trade and market in the early empires*, edited by K. Polanyi et al. Chicago: Henry Regnery.

Papandreau, Andreas G. 1943. "The location and scope of the entrepreneurial function." Ph.D. dissertation, Harvard University.

Penrose, Edith. 1959. *The theory of the growth of the firm.* New York:
John Wiley and Sons.

Pigou, A. C. 1929. *Industrial fluctuations.* 2d ed. London: Macmillan.

————. 1949. *Employment and equilibrium.* 2d ed. London: Macmillan.

Plant, Arnold. 1937. "Centralise or decentralise?" in *Selected economic
essays and addresses.* London: Routledge and Kegan Paul.

Quesnay, François. 1888. *Oeuvres economiques et philosophiques,*
edited by A. Oncken. Frankfurt: M. J. Baer.

Redlich, Fritz. 1957. "Towards a better theory of risk." *Explorations
in Entrepreneurial History* 10: 33-39.

————. 1966. "Toward the understanding of an unfortunate legacy."
Kyklos 19: 709-16.

Reekie, W. D. 1984. *Markets, entrepreneurs and liberty: An Austrian
view of capitalism.* New York: St. Martin's Press.

Riedel, A. F. J. 1838-42. *Nationalökonomie oder Volkswirthschaft
Dargestellt,* 3 vols. Berlin: F. H. Morin.

Roberts, Edward B., and Herbert A. Wainer. 1971. "Some characteristics of technical entrepreneurs." *IEEE Transactions on Engineer-
ing Management* EM-18: 100-109.

Rossini, Frederick, and Barry Bozeman. 1977. "National strategies for
technological innovation." *Administration and Society* 9: 81-
110.

Rothbard, Murray N. 1985. "Professor Hébert on entrepreneurship,"
Journal of Libertarian Studies 7: 281-286.

Rothschild, Michael and Joseph E. Stiglitz. 1976. "An essay in the economics of imperfect information." *Quarterly Journal of Economics* 90: 629-650.

Routh, Guy. 1975. *The origin of economic ideas.* White Plains, NY: International Arts and Science Press.

Rubin, Paul. 1978. "The theory of the firm and the structure of the
franchise contract," *Journal of Law and Economics* 21: 223-
233.

Sass, Stephen A. 1978. "Entrepreneurial historians and history: An
essay in organized intellect." Ph.D. dissertation, Johns Hopkins
University.

Say, J. B. 1840. *Cours complet d'economie politique pratique.* 2d ed.
Paris: Guillaumin.

———. 1845. *A treatise on political economy*. 4th ed., translated by C. R. Prinsep. Philadelphia: Grigg & Elliot.

Schon, Donald A. 1963. "Champions for radical new inventions." *Harvard Business Review* 2: 77–86.

———. 1976. *Technology and change: The new Heraclitus*. New York: Delacorte Press.

Schultz, Theodore W. 1975. "The value of the ability to deal with disequilibria." *Journal of Economic Literature* 13: 827–846.

———. 1980. "Investment in entrepreneurial ability." *Scandinavian Journal of Economics* 82: 437–448.

Schumpeter, Joseph A. 1928. "The instability of capitalism." *Economic Journal* 38: 361–386.

———. 1934. *The theory of economic development*. Translated by R. Opie from the 2nd German edition [1926]. Cambridge: Harvard University Press.

———. 1939. *Business cycles*. New York: McGraw-Hill.

———. 1947. "The creative response in economic history." *Journal of Economic History* 7: 149–159.

———. 1950. *Capitalism, socialism and democracy*, 3rd ed. New York: Harper & Row.

———. 1954. *History of economic analysis*, edited by E. B. Schumpeter. New York: Oxford University Press.

———. 1965. "Economic theory and entrepreneurial history." In *Explorations in enterprise*, edited by Hugh G. J. Aitken, pp. 45–64. Cambridge, MA: Harvard University Press.

Shackle, G. L. S. 1955. *Uncertainty in economics*. Cambridge: Cambridge University Press.

———. 1966. *The nature of economic thought*. Cambridge: Cambridge University Press.

———. 1974. *Keynesian kaleidics*. Edinburgh (Scotland): Edinburgh University Press.

Shove, G. F. 1942. "The place of Marshall's 'Principles' in the development of economic theory." *Economic Journal* 52: 294–329.

Silver, A. David. 1985. *Entrepreneurial Megabucks: The 100 Greatest Entrepreneurs of the Last Twenty-Five Years*. New York: John Wiley & Sons.

Smith, Adam. 1937. *The wealth of nations*. New York: Random House.

Souder, William E. 1981. "Encouraging entrepreneurship in the large corporation." *Research Management* 24: 18–21.

Spengler, Joseph J. 1949. Discussion to "Possibilities for a realistic theory of entrepreneurship." *American Economic Review* 39: 352–356.

―――. 1959. "Adam Smith's theory of economic growth–Part II." *Southern Economic Journal* 26: 1–12.

―――. 1960. "Richard Cantillon: First of the moderns." In *Essays in economic thought: Aristotle to Marshall*, edited by J. J. Spengler and W. R. Allen. Chicago: Rand McNally, pp. 105–140.

Spengler, Joseph J. and William R. Allen, eds. 1960. *Essays in economic thought: Aristotle to Marshall*. Chicago: Rand McNally.

Stauss, James H. 1944. "The entrepreneur: The firm." *Journal of Political Economy* 52: 112–127.

Stigler, George J. 1976. "The xistence of x-efficiency." *American Economic Review* 66: 213–216.

Streissler, Erich. 1972. "To what extent was the Austrian School marginalist?" *History of Political Economy* 4: 426–441.

Sweeney, Gerry. 1985. "Innovation is entrepreneur-led," in *Innovation policies: An international perspective*, ed. G. Sweeney. New York: St. Martin's Press.

Taussig, F. W. 1915. *Principles of economics*, rev. ed., vol. II. New York: Macmillan.

Thünen, J. H. von. 1960. *The isolated state in relation to agriculture and political economy*, vol. 2, translated by B. W. Dempsey. In *The frontier wage*, by B. W. Dempsey. Chicago: Loyola University Press, pp. 187–368.

Turgot, A. R. J. 1977. *The Economics of A. R. J. Turgot*, edited and translated by P. D. Groenewegen. The Hague: Martinus Nijhoff.

Tuttle, Charles A. 1927. "The entrepreneur function in economic literature." *Journal of Political Economy* 35: 501–521.

Usher, A. P. 1954. *A history of mechanical inventions*. Cambridge, MA: Harvard University Press.

―――. 1955. "Technical change and capital formation." In *Capital formation and economic growth*, pp. 523–550. New York: National Bureau of Economic Research.

Walker, Amasa. 1866. *The science of wealth*. Boston: Little, Brown.

Walker, Donald A. 1986. "Walras' theory of the entrepreneur," *De Economist* 134: 1–24.

Walker, Francis A. 1876. *The wages question*. New York: Henry Holt.

―――. 1884. *Political economy*. New York: Henry Holt.

————. 1887. "The source of business profits," *Quarterly Journal of Economics* 1: 265-288.

————. 1888. "A reply to Mr. Macvane: On the source of business profits," *Quarterly Journal of Economics* 2: 263-296.

Walras, Léon. [1954]. *Elements of pure economics.* Translated by W. Jaffé. Homewood, IL: Richard D. Irwin, Inc.

————. 1965. *Correspondence of Léon Walras and related papers*, 3 vols., edited by W. Jaffé. Amsterdam: North-Holland Press.

Weber, Max. 1930. *The Protestant ethic and the spirit of capitalism*, translated by Talcott Parsons. New York: Scribner's.

White, L. H. 1976. "Entrepreneurship, imagination and the question of equilibration." Manuscript.

Wicksell, Knut. [1893]. *Value, capital and rent.* English translation. London: George Allen & Unwin, 1954.

Wieser, Friedrich von. 1927. *Social economics*, translated by A. F. Hindrichs. New York: Adelphi.

Williamson, Oliver E. 1975. *Markets and hierarchies.* New York: The Free Press.

Zrinyi, Joseph. 1962. "Entrepreneurial behavior in economic theory: An historical and analytical approach." Ph.D. dissertation, Georgetown University.

INDEX OF NAMES

ABOUT THE AUTHORS

ROBERT F. HÉBERT is the Benjamin & Roberta Russell Foundation Professor of Entrepreneurial Studies at Auburn University. He is the coauthor, with Robert B. Ekelund, of a popular economics text entitled *A History of Economic Theory and Method* (2d ed., 1983) and has lectured in the United States, Europe and Great Britain. His research articles have appeared in *Quarterly Journal of Economics, Economica, Southern Economic Journal, Economic Inquiry, Journal of Public Economics*, and *History of Political Economy*, among others. He has also contributed to a number of edited volumes in the history of economics.

Dr. Hébert holds a B.S., M.S., and Ph.D. from Louisiana State University, Baton Rouge, Louisiana. He has been on the faculty at Clemson University and a member of the economics faculty at Auburn University since 1974.

ALBERT N. LINK is Professor of Economics and department head at the University of North Carolina at Greensboro. He has written extensively in the area of innovation and technological change. Recent works have appeared in such journals as the *American Economic Review*, *Journal of Political Economy*, and *Bell Journal of Economics*. He is author or co-author of eight books, the most recent being *Strategies for Technology-based Competition: Meeting the New Global Challenge*.

Dr. Link holds a B.S. (1971) in mathematics from the University of Richmond and a Ph.D. (1976) in economics from Tulane University. He has been on the faculty at UNCG since 1982. Previously, he was at Auburn University and has been visiting professor at the Maxwell School at Syracuse University.